W9-BVW-489

The Desk and Beyond:
Next Generation Reference Services

edited by

Sarah K. Steiner
and M. Leslie Madden

Association of College and Research Libraries
A division of the American Library Association
Chicago, 2008

The paper used in this publication meets the minimum requirements of American National Standard for Information Sciences-Permanence of Paper for Printed Library Materials, ANSI Z39.48-1992.∞

Library of Congress Cataloging-in-Publication Data

The desk and beyond : next generation reference services / edited by Sarah K. Steiner and M. Leslie Madden.
  p. cm.
Includes bibliographical references.
  ISBN 978-0-8389-0964-5 (pbk. : alk. paper) 1. Academic libraries--Reference services--United States. 2. Electronic reference services (Libraries)--United States. 3. Internet in library reference services--United States. 4. Library information desks--United States. 5. Reference services (Libraries)--Forecasting. 6. Reference librarians--Effect of technological innovations on. I. Steiner, Sarah K. II. Madden, M. Leslie.

Z675.U5D425 2008
025.5'2--dc22
2008004797

Copyright ©2008 by the American Library Association.
All rights reserved except those which may be granted by Sections 107 and 108 of the Copyright Revision Act of 1976.

Printed in the United States of America.

12 11 10 09 08 5 4 3 2 1

Table of Contents

Introduction

What does it mean to be an academic librarian who works from behind the desk...
and beyond? How can we take the physical reference mainstay that was a product
of the Industrial and Information Ages of the past and successfully move it into the
Conceptual Age of the present? In the late nineteenth century the reference desk
was established as the central point of library services and patron interaction, and
for over a century it remained largely unchallenged. A hundred years later, amidst
an influx of new technologies, a desire to provide more and better services, and
a growing concern that reference desks were becoming obsolete, librarians began
reevaluating reference services. In his seminal article, *What's Wrong with Reference*
(1984), William Miller called for a reexamination and reorganization of reference
services and with that, the reference-reform movement began. In 1990, Brandeis
University Library took up the challenge by dramatically eliminating its reference
desk. It was replaced by an information desk staffed by graduate students, while
librarians monitored a "Research Consultation Service Office" where patrons
with complex or lengthy questions could be referred (Massey-Burzio 1992).
The library world took notice. Librarians at other libraries began experimenting
with tiered and roving reference, but what did all of this ultimately mean for the
profession at large? Librarians (most notably Jerry Campbell[1]) have continued to
call for reference reforms, but arguably, very little has changed. There were some
significant results of the movement; they include alternative staffing (where both
paraprofessionals and librarians share desk time), experimentation with newer
technologies, and a focus on patron-centered service. Even so, predictions that
this redesign of reference services would alter the profession forever did not come
to pass (Tyckoson 1999, 60). Most libraries kept their reference desks and stayed
with the traditional model of reference service.

The emergence of the World Wide Web, however, had an impact on reference
services and librarianship in ways that could never have been predicted. Suddenly,
patrons could receive reference assistance via e-mail, and later, by chat and instant
messaging. No longer was the physical library the beginning and end-point for
research and reference assistance; patrons could check facts and perform research
from their home computers. Search engines, commercial vendors, and Web sites
became the library's main competitors. Mega-bookstores drew away library customers with comfortable seating and cafes. As the twentieth century drew to a
close, it became increasingly evident that libraries would have to change to remain
competitive. Libraries began offering space to other units on campus, restructuring
workspaces for collaborative learning, and adding more technology. Librarians
began to harness new social technologies such as chat, wikis, and blogs to reach
users. Many libraries opened coffee shops and cafes of their own.

In 2007, the debate about the importance of a physical desk returned with a vengeance. Its necessity was hotly debated at both the American Library Association Midwinter conference and the Reference Services Symposium at Columbia University Library (Bell 2007). Opponents of the traditional reference desk model argued that Millennial students, and the generations coming after them, are less likely than students in previous generations to make use of the services provided at a physical desk and that library resources should be directed toward more forward thinking services. Proponents of the reference desk model agree that reference services are evolving (and will continue to evolve) to meet the needs of future generations, but that face-to-face contact is still a powerful and important facet of the research process.

Librarians are already attempting to "go where the users are," so what are the next steps in reaching them and providing reference assistance? Over the years academic librarians have continued to explore new and innovative service methods; some small-scale, others sweeping. Some of these changes gain widespread acceptance, while others are tested and abandoned. *The Desk and Beyond* is intended to provide a thorough exploration of the present and possible future applications of eleven of the most promising new reference delivery methods. In order to reflect the growing role of the digital environment while still respecting the importance of in-person interaction, a balance of physical and virtual methods has been maintained in the book. The opening chapters (by Barratt and Daniels, Johnson and Alexander, Jastram and Zawistoski, and LaBaugh) explore in-person interactions with patrons, while later chapters (by Mathews, Landis, Boeninger, Veldof, Farkas, Francoeur, and Russell) focus on ways in which we can reach our patrons beyond the desk. The final two chapters, by Stover and Ander and Strittmatter, investigate ways to effectively market the services that we develop and to train the staff who provide those services. In-person services have always been and continue to be integral—whether your desk service supports your virtual and external programs or vice versa is up to you.

This book is intended to provide inspiration for potential reference services at your library; each chapter provides an introduction to an innovative service concept and an annotated list of sources for additional research. In the spirit of the traditional leadership role of libraries, it is the editors' hope that these ideas will bolster your own sense of discovery and pioneering for the future of libraries.

A note on the text

In order to preserve readability, the term "librarian" has been used throughout the text to denote all library staff.

Works Cited

Bell, S. (2007). Who needs a reference desk? *Library Issues: Briefings for Faculty and Administrators*. 27 (6).

Massey-Burzio, V. (1992). Reference encounters of a different kind: A symposium. *The Journal of Academic Librarianship*. 18 (5): 276-286.

Miller, W. (1984). What's wrong with reference: Coping with success and failure at the reference desk. *American Libraries.* 15 (5): 303-306, 321-322.

Tyckoson, D.A. (1999). What's right with reference. *American Libraries.* 30 (5): 57-63.

Notes

1. See Campbell, J. (1992). Shaking the conceptual foundations of reference: A perspective. *Reference Services Review.* 20 : 29-35. and Campbell, J. (2000). Clinging to traditional reference services. *Reference & User Services Quarterly.* 39 (3): 229.

Acknowledgements

Sarah's Acknowledgements

First I'd like to thank Brian Mathews, who first asked me to be involved with this project and contributed greatly to its planning and initial stages. Kathryn Deiss, our ACRL contact, has provided much assistance, patience, and kindness throughout this process. I'd also like to thank Leslie for her infinite patience, pleasantness, and good judgment, and my husband Eric for his moral support. Perhaps most importantly, I'd like to acknowledge the contributions and patience of all the contributors.

Leslie's Acknowledgements

Thank you to Brian Mathews for sending this opportunity our way and Kathryn Deiss of ACRL for her invaluable advice and speedy replies to our numerous questions. Thanks also to Sarah Steiner, my co-editor, for her sharp eyes, her sense of humor, and for inviting me to be a part of this project. Many thanks to the contributors for their hard work and dedication. Thank you to my husband Bill, and my children Claudia and Julian, for their love and support during this process. Finally, thank you to Don Frank, my mentor and friend, for always encouraging me to reach higher.

CHAPTER 1

What is Common about Learning Commons? A Look at the Reference Desk in This Changing Environment

Tim Daniels and Caroline Cason Barratt

When was the first time you heard the phrase "Information Commons"? A recent search of the *Oxford English Dictionary* online for the origin of this expression yielded no matches; however, the database did offer two words in its place: "information fatigue." Perhaps this serendipitous moment tells us something about the influx of new phrases that have come about in an attempt to accurately describe the changing landscape of our libraries and our new approaches to traditional reference service. Whether you call this phenomenon virtual reference, Library 2.0, or the cybrary, our sometimes ambivalent relationship to the ever-growing arena of technology is now firmly established as part of our post-Millennial existence. From the printing press to the podcast, libraries and library services have responded to developments in technology. In the technology-rich environment of the Learning Commons we may wonder how changes in technology and attitudes towards patron needs have had an impact on the old library mainstay—the reference desk.

It should be noted that the terms Learning Commons and Information Commons are sometimes used interchangeably; however in this chapter we will follow the distinction made by Don Beagle in *The Information Commons Handbook*, "…an Information Commons can be defined as a cluster of network access point[s] and associated IT tool[s] situated in the context of physical, digital, human, and social resources organized in support of learning" (Beagle 2007, xviii). He goes on to say that when the resources of the Information Commons are "organized in collaboration with learning initiatives sponsored by other academic units, or aligned with learning outcomes defined through a cooperative process the IC has passed a phase transition to what might more accurately called a Learning Commons or Collaboration Center" (xviii).

In the spirit of Web 2.0 collectivity, the authors surveyed their colleagues from academic libraries across the country in order to learn more about their opinions of current and future trends in reference services in the Information and Learning Commons environment.

Background

The Information Commons sprang from many changes both within and outside of academic libraries. Mary Ellen Spencer notes the advent of the "library as place" movement of the early 1990s as being part of the trend to re-examine the services and environment offered within these academic spaces (Spencer 2006, 244). The rising popularity of retail bookstores like Borders and Barnes & Noble offered a new paradigm for the use of materials typically found in academic libraries. People flocked to these bookstores to read books and magazines while nestled in comfortable armchairs, to meet friends to chat over cappuccino, and to participate in community events. Patrons seemed to prefer these cozy and informal spaces to traditional library buildings, and libraries soon began making alterations in response to declining gate counts (Spencer 2006; Gardner and Eng 2005; and others). The acceptance of food and drink within the library was only one addition that challenged old policies and identities; the collaborative and conversational areas modeled by bookstores also challenged libraries to define similar spaces and soon more room was opened for conversation and group seating. The quiet, monastic study hall environment was still present and in demand in academic libraries, but many patrons appreciated the option to use the library space in a slightly different way—as a place to meet friends, to collaborate, and to stay a while.

In addition to these environmental changes, academic librarians have continued to explore new ways to employ emerging technologies in patron interactions. In other words, the library's physical transformation into a Learning Commons has not been the only alteration to come about in response to changes in patrons' needs and developments in technology. Reference librarians, too, are using technology in more sophisticated and varied ways. Social networking software like *Facebook* and *MySpace*, instant messaging, blogs, and RSS feeds are just a few ways librarians have employed Web 2.0 technology to perform traditional reference tasks.

Bernard Frischer recognizes this phenomenon in his essay, "The Ultimate Internet Café." Frischer identifies three major consequences of digital technology on the research library and says that, "… the research library will be special not so much because of the quantity of information it can offer but of the quality of the experience in which that information is presented" (Frischer 2005, 40). Indeed, many academic libraries have risen to the challenge by devoting large amounts of time and money towards planning a learning environment that includes an array of productivity software presented on upgraded computers within newly furnished and renovated spaces. Libraries complement these user-centered tools by offering traditional reference services using new technologies and by providing technology support in addition to bibliographic assistance. These spaces are often reinventions of old reference rooms, but by infusing them with digital technology, collaborative work areas, and computer services, planners have created a learning environment that approaches student needs in a new way. The presentation of these expanded services and resources has become as important as providing the tools themselves. It is the combination of the two that generates collaborative learning and that fosters an environment that is perhaps better described as a Learning Commons than just one that provides Information. Merely adding computers to a library does not make it a Learning Commons; it is necessary to offer the space to patrons in a collaborative, more flexible environment while retaining the customer service that patrons have come to expect at their library. In order to provide inclusive service in the Learning Commons, traditional functions such as reference are combined with technology support in order to give the patron complete support.

While Web 2.0 is still the Internet, the Learning Commons is still the library—but with a difference. A few of the most marked characteristics of Web 2.0 are the emphasis on social interaction, the ability to collaborate and add to existing knowledge, and the flexibility to tailor information to suit one's particular needs. If we view the Learning Commons as the physical embodiment of many of these Web 2.0 characteristics, we can see it as a social space, a collaborative space, a process-oriented space, and a changing space. The reference desk within the Commons is also in transition. By examining where we are now in relation to the physical "desk" and our work behind and beyond it, we are provided with a picture of current trends and an image of our possible future.

Methodology

The authors administered a survey to create a current environmental scan in order to determine how various libraries and librarians viewed reference within the Learning Commons model. A survey consisting of seventeen questions was created using an online survey tool (Zoomerang.com) and was distributed through several library-related electronic mailing lists. One hundred forty seven responses were received, mostly from academic librarians at two and four-year institutions.

Demographic Breakdown of Respondents

Type of Library	Number
Two Year Community College	10
College	22
University	107

Almost three-quarters of respondents reported an affiliation with a university library. Fifteen percent reported from a college library and seven percent from a two-year community college. Only one percent designated their library as a public library. Responses from academic libraries (university, college, and two-year college libraries) were culled from the group to provide 137 complete responses.[1]

Results

Services Offered at the Learning Commons

A unique element of most Learning Commons is the expansion of services offered both from the service desks and the Commons in general.

Services Offered at Learning Commons

Services Offered*	Number	Percentage of Total
Circulation	102	75.4%
General Information	47	34.6%
Periodicals	16	13.2%

Services Offered at Learning Commons

Services Offered*	Number	Percentage of Total
Research Support	92	83.4%
Reserves	17	12.5%
Special Formats	14	10.2%
Technology Support	66	48.2%
Tutoring	18	13.1%
*Respondents could indicate more than one category		

Many traditional library services still exist at the desk, but beyond reference assistance, one of the most popular additions to the Learning Commons desk is the availability of technology support. All include computers and computer technology ranging from the most basic software (including word processing and spreadsheets) to very sophisticated technologies (including media production and complex statistical packages). Many Commons also include various types of media production hardware. Hardware can include scanners (for print, photographs, and photographic negatives), high speed computers (both PC and Macintosh), and in some cases, sound and video recording technologies.

Libraries are also responding to the pedagogical trends in academia, most frequently to the increase of group project assignments. Many Commons provide rooms for group study and space for groups to rehearse their presentations. These practice rooms include projectors, white boards, and in some instances, the ability to record a performance for later critique. Eighteen libraries also indicated that they are working with other academic departments on campus to include tutoring services, with writing assistance being the most popular service. Some libraries are working to merge many of their services within as few desks as possible, while in other instances each service has its own support desk. These services include periodicals support, special formats, technology support, and general information. The number of desks ranges from one to ten in the respondents' libraries. For those libraries that are merging desks, technology support is common, but some academic libraries are combining their circulation and reference services at one service point.

These hybridized desks are often re-named in order to better describe the services offered. Though the "reference desk" is still frequently called by this traditional title, other names include Library Services Desk, LC Tech Desk, Technology Support Desk, and Information Station, to name a few.

Desk Names

Desk Name	Number	Percentage Reported
Reference Desk	49	39%
Information Desk	44	35%
Research Desk	15	12%
Other	70	55%

Staffing at Desk
Reference Desk Staffing at the Learning Commons
In response to the evolving Learning Commons environment, reference desk staffing is also changing. Many libraries are combining human communication skills and information technology to provide both virtual and in-person reference service to library users well beyond the confines of a stationary desk.

Staffing*	Number	Percentage Reported
Librarians	100	78%
IT Support Staff	55	43%
Library paraprofessionals	72	56%
Students	85	66%
*Respondents could indicate more than one category		

Libraries are moving away from the "just in case" model of service (i.e. always staffing the reference desk with the most highly trained librarians "just in case" someone shows up who requires their expertise) to a more practical model. Librarians have not abandoned the desk, as patrons have come to expect a high level of service from this station. Instead, librarians are meeting this demand by using a variety of personnel to provide desk services. This model can offer a single service point where the special skills and professional responsibilities of librarians are better utilized, and patrons can find help for a variety of needs. Increasingly, support is offered by highly trained non-MLIS staff. In some cases, library administration has created positions for Information or Learning Commons Librarians, a new job category for librarians who are reference generalists, but are also comfortable providing technology support. Many libraries report that technology support, mostly in the form of student assistants or staff from campus IT, make up a large number of the new support personnel added to the desks.

New Skills for a New Reference Desk
The question then becomes, "what skills do librarians need to be successful in a Learning Commons environment?" Respondents reported that technical skills are essential. Not only must staff have a working knowledge of the current products that library patrons use to complete their assignments, but they must also have an understanding of how these technologies transition over time to the next generation of production software. As has always been the case, a deep understanding of library products is also important. Many of the reference resources librarians depend on are migrating (or already have migrated) into the digital arena, and this trend will only continue. Even beyond this understanding of the development of information technologies, librarians must begin to explore how our digital resources can be embedded at the users' point of need. It is no longer sufficient to simply provide links to these resources from Web pages; we must provide access

where the user is most likely to need these tools. Presenting library resources at a users' point of need can be accomplished in several ways. Many universities are using course management software (such as *Blackboard/WebCT* or *Sakai*) where faculty routinely post assignments and readings. By partnering with faculty, librarians can create course guides that direct students to the resources that will prove to be the most useful. As discussed in the professional literature, today's students are entering college with a different set of experiences and skills (Thomas and McDonald 2005, Oblinger and James 2005, and others). In order to provide current and future generations with the skills they need to be successful, librarians must maintain a current awareness of learning theory in higher education, and of the tools and resources that students use to demonstrate their understanding of the academic material. When asked about key skills and subjects that should be taught in MLIS programs, many respondents identified technology—specifically educational technology—as important to a new librarian's success.

MLIS Programs & New Librarian Skill Sets

Skill Required*	Number	Percentage Reported
Technology Skills	119	85%
Educational Theory	90	64%
Instructional Theory	111	79%
Instructional Technology	119	85%
*Respondents could indicate more than one category		

Many respondents also felt that communication skills were vital to the success of new librarians, especially as most will find themselves working in a highly collaborative environment.

Impact of the Learning Commons on the Reference Desk

The authors' primary interest was in discovering librarians' perceptions of the effect of the Learning Commons environment on reference service.

Impact of Learning Commons on Reference Desk

Impact described*	Number	Percentage Reported
Increase in instruction[2]	24	17.5%
Increase in depth of questions	9	6.6%
Decrease in depth of questions	15	10.9%
Increase in number of questions	15	10.9%
Decrease in number of questions	16	11.7%
Increased visibility	15	10.9%
Increased traffic	12	8.8%

Impact of Learning Commons on Reference Desk

Impact described*	Number	Percentage Reported
Change in character of the library	20	14.6%
Increased services offered	13	9.5%
Increased collaboration	17	12.4%
No impact	16	11.7%
N/A (respondent did not yet have an IC)	2	1.5%

*Respondents could indicate more than one category

While the performance of electronic reference via e-mail and instant messaging software has been customary for some time, the authors surmised that the reshaping of the library space, as well as new staffing models at the reference desk, would have an impact on how reference service was performed both in terms of staffing and services offered. However, rather than describe a localized change at the desk, respondents indicated that the greatest impact that the Information Commons has had is a more generalized change in the character of the library.

Respondents commented that the more open arrangement of their reference room has revealed new sightlines throughout the space and has enhanced visibility of the reference desk and of the students making use of the Commons. This physical openness and accessibility influences the overall climate of the reference room, making collaboration amongst students and between students and library personnel more likely. Increased collaboration also includes working with other campus departments in these new spaces. Respondents found that multiple perspectives on service and an increased knowledge base occur when the desk is staffed by IT personnel as well as librarians. Also, changes in policy that were intended to alter perceptions of the library (especially regarding the allowance of food and noise) appear to have been successful. Respondents indicate that the vision behind the Learning Commons has come to fruition, and they describe these new spaces as being more in touch with student life and, for better or worse, more boisterous and active places. Many respondents also reported that the Commons has affected their roles as instructors, and that teaching has taken on a greater focus in their professional activities. As responsibility for answering questions at the desk is now often shared amongst individuals with varying areas of expertise, librarians are free to concentrate on core library research and instruction endeavors. A common refrain in the survey results is that instead of worrying about paper jams and other technical issues, librarians can concentrate on helping students with their research through consultations and by spending more time in the classroom. Although results showed an increase in the number and variety of questions, an equal number of respondents reported a decrease in the level of intellectual depth and complexity of the questions they receive. Perhaps because of this, many are finding an outlet for library instruction away from the boundaries of the reference desk.

Successes and Challenges

Respondents also commented about the successes and challenges of their Learning Commons.

Successes in the Learning Commons

Successes*	Number	Percentage Reported
Increased traffic	36	26.3%
Increase in instruction	21	15.3%
Increased services	4	2.9%
*Respondents could indicate more than one category		

The most frequently reported success is an increase in traffic to the library. The change in environment has worked to make the library a more attractive destination, and students have returned to the library to take advantage of the new services, technology, and collaborative work spaces offered there. This success has a negative side, however, and many respondents said that noise is one of the biggest challenges they have in the Commons. Respondents reported that higher noise levels hinder students' concentration on academic work and disturb librarians in consultation with students at the reference desk. Another challenge that may come from the success of the Commons model is the fear that lack of continued funding will make it difficult, if not impossible, to maintain the level of technology and staffing needed to support this new variety of services and resources.

The top challenge mentioned by respondents is clashing service philosophies between librarians and IT professionals, and sometimes between the librarians themselves.

Challenges in the Learning Commons

Challenges*	Number	Percentage Reported
Clashing philosophies (among partners)	38	27.7%
Increased noise	27	19.7%
Increased traffic	19	13.9%
Clashing philosophies (among librarians)	9	6.6%
Loss of library identity	10	7.3%
Funding facility/training	22	16.1%
*Respondents could indicate more than one category		

Responses indicate that the implementation of the Learning Commons model has been polemical in some libraries. While many librarians embrace the new emphasis on technology, integrated service desks, and a collaborative work environment, others do not enjoy working in the Commons. Also, since many Learning Commons function as joint efforts between libraries, IT departments, and other academic groups on campus, coming to an agreement on the overarching mission and identity of these spaces can be challenging. Additionally, respondents identified members of library, IT, and campus administration as having key roles in creating a collaborative work environment for the people who staff the Commons. The example they set in acting together to plan the building has a strong influence on the working relationships of their staff.

Anxieties

More than twenty-five percent of respondents cited technology in the Commons as a major source of anxiety. This percentage rate is more than double the rate for any other reported anxiety.

Anxieties Concerning the Learning Commons

Anxiety*	Number	Percentage Reported
Negative change in librarians' status	10	7.3%
Librarians are not needed	14	10.2%
Identity of librarians/library	11	8.0%
Loss of control over library	16	11.7%
Problems with the partnership	7	5.1%
Technology	35	25.5%
Change	11	8.0%
Too much work	11	8.0%
No anxiety	15	10.9%

*Respondents could indicate more than one category

Respondents cited apprehension about keeping staff technology skills up to date to effectively assist students with productivity software and other technology. Sufficient technology training for librarians and technical support staff at the desk may alleviate this fear. Supervisors should consider making continuing education programs a standard part of staff planning in these environments. An additional concern relates to funding. As these new spaces age, will library workers be able to acquire the monetary resources necessary to refresh their computers and software, and ultimately, maintain the Commons' standing as technological centers of campus? As librarians collaborate with other non-library departments, some respondents are concerned about a diminishing level of control over what happens in the Learning Commons. Sharing space requires sharing a philosophy of how that space should be used, and respondents who enjoy a successful cooperative work environment may find that services or building uses evolve naturally over time. Ranked third in responses was that there had been no anxiety at all, and that the Learning Commons model was working well without much worry beyond the usual growing pains of significant change.

Conclusion

Just as the university is often described as a microcosm of the world beyond its campus borders, so the Learning Commons is a microcosm of the university. The library now may embody the classrooms, computing centers, student social spaces, and academic departments that were traditionally beyond the library's walls. The Learning Commons is truly a physical representation of the Web 2.0 dynamic: it is a social space, a collaborative space, a process-oriented space, and a changing space. In this environment, libraries are challenged to provide not only traditional reference service, but also to offer services that in the past have been seen as outside the realm of a library's purview. In order to meet this challenge, we must not only continue to provide excellent reference service at our physical service points, but we must also take our skills into the social environment of our campuses. By being involved with freshmen experience programs, attending student government events, hosting library gaming nights, providing in person reference in departments and dorms, and attending other social events, librarians can interact with students and faculty and begin to build community. Librarians may also find that they develop new skills that will allow them to provide access beyond the desk in both the physical and virtual world. By following a Learning Commons model, libraries can develop strategic partnerships that will bring to the library the campus services that students need to complete assignments and produce successful projects. As this new environment continues to change, we must be mindful not to rest on our accomplishments, but to use these successes to build confidence, develop new services, and acquire new skills.

Sources for Additional Research

Beagle, D. 2006. *The Information Commons Handbook.* New York: Neal-Schuman Publishers.

> In this book the author describes not only what an Information Commons is but also the roles of the Information Commons in academic libraries. The book also covers the practical aspects of planning for and designing an Information Commons.

Bennett, S. 2007. First questions for designing higher education learning spaces. *Journal of Academic Librarianship* 33 (1): 14-26.

> In this article, the author suggests six foundational questions that all colleges and universities should ask when designing a learning space. These questions focus on "… the character of the learning we want to happen in the space" rather than operational or physical concerns in order to better deliver an effective environment for academic work and achievement (14). The author employs data from the National Survey on Student Engagement to support his argument.

Dallis, D., and C. Walters. 2006. Reference services in the commons environment. *Reference Services Review* 34 (2): 248-260.

This article describes the planning and implementation of a new Information Commons serving undergraduate students at a large research university. Authors describe, "… the effect of the Commons environment on reference services and environment and highlights the importance of a strong relationship between libraries and information technology providers in developing successful public services in an information commons" (248).

Frischer, B. 2005. The ultimate Internet café: Reflections of a practicing digital humanist about designing a future for the research library in the digital age. In *Library as Place: Rethinking Roles, Rethinking Space.* Washington, DC: Council on Library and Information Resources, 41-55.

In this article, the author imagines the library of the future and describes the role of technology in shaping the modern research library, including changes in services and physical space as well as new roles for libraries in response to advanced technology.

Gardner, S., and S. Eng. 2005. What students want: Generation Y and the changing function of the academic library. *portal: Libraries & the Academy* 5 (3): 405-420.

This article discusses the results of a survey of undergraduate students in 2003. The survey polled these students and asked questions regarding library service and user expectation. The authors use the survey as a study of members of generation Y and attempt to predict what services will need to be expanded and developed in the future.

Hein, K. K. 2006. Information uncommon: Public computing in the life of reference. *Reference Services Review* 34 (1): 33-42.

This author describes the new roles taken by reference librarians in an attempt to provide service for new technology at a traditional desk. The article provides an overview of both space and personnel management while offering observations that may inform a best practice model for reference desks in an academic library's Information Commons.

Lippincott, J. K. 2004. New library facilities: Opportunities for collaboration. *Resource Sharing & Information Networks* 17 (1): 147-157.

This article discusses how libraries that are going through a building or remodeling project can and should collaborate with other campus units to provide a holistic set of services to library patrons.

MacWhinnie, L. A. 2003. The information commons: The academic library of the future. *portal: Libraries & the Academy* 3 (2): 241.

MacWhinnie reviews Information Commons in the Unites States and Canada to provide a snapshot of their guiding principles and special features, and offers an assessment of each building's strengths and challenges.

Oblinger, D.G. ed. 2006. *Learning Spaces.* Educause. http://www.educause.edu/learningspaces.

This collection of essays explores the philosophical underpinnings of user centered learning spaces, focusing on "… how learner expectations influence such spaces, the principles and activities that facilitate learning, and the role of technology from the perspective of those who create learning environments." The e-book also includes thirty case studies from "innovative learning spaces" throughout the US, with international examples as well.

Oblinger, D.G. and L. James eds. 2005. *Educating the Net Generation*. Educause. http://www.educause.edu/educatingthenetgen.

This collection of essays examines the impact of the Net Generation on higher education. Over all, the work looks at the skills and experiences of the Net Generation and how these factors impact their expectations when they ar rive on campus. The book also discusses the use of technology in teaching these students.

Spencer, M. E. 2006. Evolving a new model: The information commons. *Reference Services Review* 34 (2): 242-247.

This article tracks the development of the idea of the Information Commons. The author examines reference service, user expectations, and planning. Suggestions for future developments and expansion of the Information Commons model are made. The article also includes URLs for examples of libraries with Information Commons areas.

Thomas, C. and R. H. McDonald. 2005. Millennial net value(s): Disconnects between libraries and the information age mindset. *Proceedings of the Free Culture & the Digital Library Symposium*, Emory University, Atlanta, GA October 2005. http://dscholarship.lib.fsu.edu/general/4/.

In this article the authors examine the impact of Net Generation on Libraries. The authors suggest that this emerging group of library users have an expectation that information will be integrated into their electronic environments. The article examines how libraries can develop tools and strategies to support the needs of this and other generations of users.

Van Scoyoc, A. M. and C. Cason [Barratt]. 2006. The electronic academic library: Undergraduate research behavior in a library without books. *portal: Libraries and the Academy* 6 (1): 47-58.

This study examines undergraduate research behavior in a strictly electronic library environment. The authors surveyed students to discover what resources they relied on when performing research in this new library. The authors find that students rely primarily on Internet sites and material in their online instruction modules for their research needs. The authors discuss possible reasons for these findings, new pedagogical practices as indicated by the results, and define areas for further research

Works Cited

Beagle, D. 2006. *The Information Commons Handbook*. New York: Neal-Schuman Publishers.

Frischer, B. 2005. "The ultimate Internet café: Reflections of a practicing digital humanist about designing a future for the research library in the digital age." In *Library as Place: Rethinking Roles, Rethinking Space*. Washington, DC: Council on Library and Information Resources: 41-55.

Gardner, S., and S. Eng. 2005. What students want: Generation Y and the changing function of the academic library. *portal: Libraries & the Academy* 5 (3): 405-420.

Oblinger, D. G. ed. 2006. *Learning Spaces*. Educause, http://www.educause.edu/learningspaces.

Oblinger, D. G. and L. James eds. 2005. *Educating the Net Generation*. Educause. http://www.educause.edu/educatingthenetgen.

Spencer, M. E. 2006. Evolving a new model: The information commons. *Reference Services Review* 34 (2): 242-247.

Thomas, C. and R. H. McDonald. 2005. Millennial net value(s): Disconnects Between libraries and the information age mindset. *Proceedings of the Free Culture & the Digital Library Symposium*, Emory University, Atlanta, GA October 2005 http://dscholarship.lib.fsu.edu/general/4/.

Notes

1. Three of the seventeen questions were open-ended and required a numeric categorization in order to tabulate them using statistical software (SPSS). The authors coded these free text responses by assigning a response category (i.e. Anxiety—Status, Anxiety – Collaboration) and the value of "yes," "no," or "skip." If a respondent did not expressly mention a particular anxiety category, that was marked as "no"; if they did, that answer was marked as "yes"; and if the respondent skipped this question altogether, that was marked "skip." As free text responses could be categorized in more than one area, percentages will not add up to one hundred.

2. An increase in instruction was the highest reported result, and no one reported a decrease in instruction due to changing from a traditional to a Learning Commons environment.

CHAPTER 2

Personalizing the Library via Research Consultations

Iris Jastram and Ann Gwinn Zawistoski

In these days of rapid change, the buzz words "Web 2.0" and "Library 2.0" fly around the library community seeding discussions with ideas of newness and technological advance. Libraries are embracing tools and services that allow individual researchers to define how their interfaces look, where they want information delivered, how they want to organize that information, and when all of this work should take place. But while the concepts of Web 2.0 and Library 2.0 have implications for technology, they are fundamentally about reaffirming the importance of the patron and recommitting to the needs of the individual researcher. As Casey and Savastinuk write, "Any service, physical or virtual, that successfully reaches users, is evaluated frequently, and makes use of customer input is a Library 2.0 service" (Casey and Savastinuk 2006, 42). The key, they say, is "user-centered change" (40).

With the increase of interdisciplinary and multidisciplinary study in the academy, and with more and more factual information readily available on the Internet, the type of assistance researchers need is shifting. Six years ago, Donald Frank and his colleagues pointed out that "dramatic increases in interdisciplinary research have combined with technological developments and changes in scholarly communication to fuel the need for information consulting in academic libraries (Frank 2001, 92). Four years ago, David Tyckoson noted that the demand for fact-based reference help was decreasing and would continue to diminish (Tyckoson 2003, 15). In response to these trends, traditional reference desk service has shifted from being the cornerstone of academic research services to being one in a suite of services designed to serve today's researchers more nimbly and robustly. In this context, other research services, like individual research consultations, augment reference services and move us toward revitalized research services.

Called variously "consultations" and "clinics" in the library literature (and "appointments" at the authors' college), consultations not only allow for more individualized interactions, but they also resonate with the most prevalent method of one-on-one academic assistance on a college or university campus—faculty office hours. Individual research consultations, like faculty office hours, offer time and space for researchers to grapple with pressing research needs, to increase their understanding of those needs, and to develop strategies for overcoming these and future research challenges. This analogy also encourages those in the academic community to see consultations as a natural fit on campus, and it contributes to a sense of collaboration between librarians and teaching faculty.

In addition to greater personalization and ties to academic patterns of assistance, consultations complement other reference services by increasing the amount of time researchers can spend working with librarians. In their study, "Quality Reference Service: A Preliminary Case Study," Stalker and Murfin found that sufficient time spent with patrons at the reference desk was a major factor in increasing the number of successful reference interactions beyond the standard rate of fifty-five percent (Stalker and Murfin 1996, 427-28). Consultations allow longer periods of uninterrupted time than are normally possible at the desk, and by extension, they are more likely to result in successful outcomes. Moreover, offering both reference and consultation services streamlines the reference workflow and relieves reference librarians from the pressure of fully answering every question that comes to the desk. If questions become highly complex, begin to take significant time (particularly if the reference service is very busy), or seem to require the help of a librarian who is an expert in a particular field or resource, reference librarians can easily refer researchers to a consulting librarian. In this way, consultations offer a way to expand reference interactions into full-fledged, point-of-need, individualized assistance.

Offering consultations is not a new idea; it has been tried by small colleges and large universities alike. In the late 1970s, Berea College began offering individual research tutorials as a substitute for classroom instruction in one key freshman course (Hughes and Flandreau 1980). Librarians there facilitated student learning by offering individualized, point-of-need, hands-on, course-integrated instruction. Later, hoping to offer a service for every type of research need and remain cost effective without sacrificing quality, William Whitson (1995) advocated including consultations as one of a set of differentiated services. More recently, an e-mail inquiry sent to library e-mail discussion lists revealed numerous consultation programs that are flourishing across the nation.[1] The recent library literature has also included accounts of successful programs at small liberal arts colleges, such as Cornell College (Donham and Green 2004), as well as descriptions of programs at libraries in large university systems (Yi 2003). Highlighting the implications of institutional differences, Catherine Cardwell of Bowling Green State University, Katherine Furlong of Lafayette College, and Julie O'Keeffe of Marquette University describe their institutions' differing consultation programs (Cardwell, Furlong, and O'Keeffe 2001). Based on the literature, all of these implementations share a common theme: "To reach new users and better serve current ones through customer-driven offerings" (Casey and Savastinuk 2006, 40).

Promoting Learning, Building Trust

Michelle Holschuh Simmons writes compellingly about the librarian's unique position as a simultaneous insider and outsider in the academic environment and about how this position can enable rich learning among undergraduates. Scholars in their fields, she argues, are so familiar with their processes that they are no longer aware of the decisions they make and the discourses that they employ. Librarians, as insider/outsiders, can recognize these decisions and discourses as the conventions that they are and can therefore reveal them to students (Simmons 2005, 298). In this way, according to Simmons, librarians contribute to the primary goal of an undergraduate education by helping to initiate students into the discourse of their chosen fields (304).

We believe that this line of reasoning applies even more broadly, extending beyond discourses to include the disciplinary knowledge that feeds search strategies and results-list evaluation. In our discussions with faculty members about their students' research abilities, the faculty members expressed variations on a common theme in statements such as, "My student was struggling to find sources, but I entered a couple words into the search box and instantly brought back relevant results." The faculty members, scholars in their fields, were drawing on their vast schemata of prior experience to pick out relevant search terms and strategies. Students lack access to these internal roadmaps of terms, authors, and methodologies. Similarly, scholars exploring unfamiliar or multidisciplinary topics may also struggle to find appropriate resources and may benefit from working with a consulting librarian to identify key authors and terms. The librarian can lead the researchers, be they students or experts, through the iterative process of discovering the key terms, important authors, and distinguishing methodologies associated with a topic. In this case, the fact that the librarian is not as specialized as a scholar in a particular field of study becomes a pedagogical advantage.

While the reference desk is often a site of this kind of dynamic learning (Beck and Turner 2001; Elmborg 2002; Fox 1998), consultation sessions allow librarians and researchers to engage in collaborative learning experiences that are difficult to maintain at the desk. During these sessions, librarians and researchers work together to generate search terms, thumb through bibliographies, note citations to look up, and navigate Web pages and bibliographic databases. As the sense of collaboration between the librarian and the researcher builds, both can feel more comfortable "thinking out loud" so that each learns from the other's decision-making processes. Paced according to the researcher's needs, consultations may even stretch over several meetings. In these cases, researchers leave the initial session with a follow-up appointment scheduled or with encouragement to come back if fresh confusions arise. The possibility of future sessions reinforces the concept that the research process is not a linear advance toward an answer; it is a particularized and iterative process in which each new strategy is built on the successes and failures of prior strategies. In short, the personalized and collaborative nature of individual research consultations encourages the kind of educational interaction that James Elmborg advocates, which combines the "authentic process of discovery," rooted in a real and immediate research need, with the time and space to expand "the most dynamic teaching position in the academy" beyond the reference desk (Elmborg 2002, 459 and 463).

Removing Barriers: Offering Assistance on the Researcher's Terms

These days it is common in academic libraries to speak of the physical and psychological barriers that reference desks pose for approaching patrons. Libraries have experimented with various remedies ranging from discarding the desk (Sonntag and Palsson 2007) to increasing its height so as to maintain equal eye levels between the librarian and the researcher (Warnement 2003, 82). Reference desks are well-suited to people who think their questions are best asked on a drop-in basis or those who appreciate knowing that help is available at a predictable location. They are also convenient for people under extreme deadlines who cannot wait to schedule a consultation. Consultations, however, are ideal for anxious researchers and individuals with complex research needs. The added privacy of working with a librarian (either in the librarian's office or in some other designated consulting area) may protect patrons from feeling that their ignorance is on public display.

The time, space, privacy, and trust afforded by consultations also removes the burden of forming "reference-ready" questions, a potentially serious barrier for researchers who may not have well-formed ideas about what they cannot find or do on their own. We have observed that researchers often explore more nascent and undefined ideas during consultations than they do at the desk. Requests for consultations are often pleas for help getting started on or help determining the feasibility of a topic. Consultations offer an accommodating space, however, for those who feel their questions are too nebulous for quick answers or who prefer the familiarity of working with a known and trusted librarian.

Implementing a Patron-Centered Consultation Service

The primary goal of a successful research consultation service is to focus on individual researchers at particular institutions. These services reject a "one size fits all" model of research assistance. Consequently, librarians may adopt significantly different consultation models, depending on their constituents, available physical and virtual space, staffing, and other local circumstances.

Key Decisions

Creating "user-centered change," as Casey and Savastinuk advocate (2006, 40), begins with the users. Determining whom to serve is therefore one of the guiding decisions that shapes consultation services. Will consulting librarians meet with students from all class years and majors, undergraduate and graduate, or with only a portion of the student population? Will they offer consultations to faculty members and administrators? Will patrons from outside of the campus community be allowed to request individualized research assistance?

Deciding whom to serve also has implications for the library as a whole. The library's position and relevance on campus depends on the good will of faculty and administrators. These groups not only "filter their perception of the library onto the student body" and "wield significant influence over student use and recognition of the library," but they also influence library budgets (Frank et al. 2001, 92-93). While working with administrators is not normally a large part of a research service, consulting librarians can lend their expertise in many ways. For example, they can help to plan and manage the committee research efforts and provide valuable research assistance to those writing speeches and reports.

At some institutions this may become one of the most powerful ways to bolster the library's relevance on campus, while at others, service to students may situate the library as a vital site of learning on campus.

The kinds of researchers who make up the service's target population, as well as librarian availability and the library's service goals, also help to determine how best to distribute consultations among the librarians. In some circumstances, it makes sense for librarians to divide the campus population among themselves (so that researchers schedule consultations with "their" librarians). On other campuses, it makes more sense to schedule consultations on the basis of librarian availability. When libraries divide the campus population by academic division, subject, class year, or even last name,[2] the librarians become somewhat analogous to academic advisors, and the researchers become accustomed to working with a particular person over the course of time. On the other hand, scheduling and work distribution are perhaps the primary advantages of the model in which requests for consultations are distributed based on the librarians' availability.[3] This type of distribution does not simply benefit librarians, however. Researchers who are not on campus every day or during traditional work hours benefit from having librarians available to assist them at the times that are most convenient.[4] No matter how consultations are distributed among the librarians, researchers should be given the option to seek out a particular librarian in certain circumstances. For example, it often makes sense for a researcher to work more than once with the same librarian over the course of a single research project. And students who have had a library instruction session benefit from the ability to schedule consultations with the librarian who led that session.

Despite the clear benefits, adding research consultations to an existing suite of services is not without its challenges. One such challenge is remaining flexible enough to accommodate researchers' diverse needs and preferences. This flexibility is critical because researchers can and will ask questions in many venues, such as during an instruction session, at the desk, around campus, or in a consultation. In addition, some researchers may be intimidated by the idea that they have to choose the "right" service or the "right" librarian before requesting help. They need access to services that mirror the level of intervention that they deem appropriate. Those looking for basic keywords for initial searches on a topic may feel ridiculous going through the trouble of scheduling a consultation. At the same time, those overwhelmed by the research process may feel that they need extended amounts of time with a librarian. These feelings are valid even if finding keywords for initial searches require extensive work or if the overwhelmed researcher simply needs to be pointed toward one gateway source. Librarians face the endeavor of providing a variety of research services that are robust and flexible enough to serve researchers even when they are uncertain about the level of assistance they need.

Though it may initially seem challenging, initiating a consultation program need not be overwhelming and is often, in fact, quite rewarding. Librarians can begin by instituting a pilot service (targeting only one class, one professor, one department, or one class year) in order to get a sense of the time and resources the service will require and to assess its impact on the library staff. As the pilot progresses, librarians will probably find that conducting research consultations is deeply satisfying. Unlike interactions at the reference desk or during instruction sessions, consultations give librarians the opportunity to watch researchers emerge slowly from a fog of confusion. Consulting librarians also have the chance to work on single questions for longer periods of time, and they can get to know researchers over the course of a project, class, or academic career. Most gratifying of all, researchers sometimes come back to show the results of their study or to say "thank you." This type of personal interaction strengthens librarians' convictions that they are integral members of the academic environment.

▨▨▨c▨*ing the Service*

The possibilities for publicizing research consultations are nearly endless. Publicity could include anything from word-of-mouth, to advertisements in campus publications, to campus-wide campaigns. The publicity itself can be quite simple as long as it is tied directly to the goals of the service (Dodsworth 1998, 320). For example, instruction librarians can encourage students to make appointments for research consultations and faculty members can refer students to consulting librarians.[5] If librarians wish to go beyond these methods, they can embark on targeted campaigns timed to reach researchers when they are likely to be worried about their research projects. Once the service is up and running, word-of-mouth advertising can become a powerful force on campus. Ideally, influential faculty members will spread the word among their departments and encourage new faculty to meet with librarians and to send their students to the library. Satisfied researchers will recommend consultations to their colleagues, friends, or roommates.

Simply being visible is also an effective marketing strategy for this type of service, which strives for personalization and approachability. Consulting librarians who teach, perform reference service, and consult are highly visible and become readily associated with research assistance on campus. Attending campus events, participating on committees, walking through departments, or having offices that are visible from the reference area are effective ways of building up this ambient visibility. If researchers recognize librarians' names and faces, they are more likely to feel that they are asking for help from a person rather than submitting questions to an institution, and this makes the library and its services seem friendly and approachable.

▨*va*▨*ating the Service*

As Casey and Savastinuk (2000) remind us, continual evaluation is important to a successful library service. The easiest method of data collection is to keep basic records about the consultations themselves. At our own library, we track information on the type of researcher, a student's class year, course number, topic, and length of consultation. From these simple data, we can track the ebb and flow of consultation requests throughout the academic year, track trends in research topics and interests, and learn which classes or departments are particularly research-intensive. Libraries can go further by distributing surveys at the end of each semester to anyone who has participated in a consultation, working with faculty members to see if students who have met with a librarian get different grades from students who have not, or including questions on information literacy surveys or course evaluations about student usage of the consulting program.[6]

Moving Forward

Local library collections are an ever-shrinking portion of the available information universe, and even these collections are moving online. With all of these resources accessible without the mediation of a reference librarian, the purpose and mission of reference services are under discussion. In her article on the future of reference, Jo Bell Whitlatch notes that the trend toward knowledge-counseling "is already changing the nature of reference services from answering the quick, routine, less than five-minute questions to a more extended counseling or coaching interaction" (Whitlatch 2003, 15). As the number of short reference questions decreases, some librarians may find that it makes sense to remove professional staff from the reference desk in response and envision it merely as a referral point designed to funnel all in-depth reference questions to one-on-one consultations. Others may find, as we have, that the success of the consultation program has not diminished the need for immediate help at the reference desk and has, in fact, encouraged more in-depth desk interactions. In our case, as the expectation of individualized research help has taken a deeper hold on our campus, many reference interactions have come to mirror mini-consultation sessions.

In the past, libraries have attempted to meet diverse research needs by instituting "differentiated services," where patrons are asked to "adjust their behavior sufficiently to allow libraries to perform their work in the most effective way" (Whitson 1995, 109). Moving forward, however, libraries are adjusting their services sufficiently to allow researchers to perform *their* work in the most effective way. Some libraries may choose to offer research consultations in conjunction with their traditional reference desk services for researchers who prefer drop-in counseling at a predictable place during predictable hours. Others may find that it makes sense to use consultations for all research assistance. Campus culture and research needs dictate what form this adjustment takes, but whether it shifts researchers away from the desk or not, its primary motivation must be local researchers' needs.

As consultation programs mature, they must adapt to continuing changes in the library landscape and in campus research habits. As they adapt, they may in turn effect changes in library operations. Unlike in standard reference services, research consultation librarians may not be in predictable places at predictable hours, and there may be significant preparation and follow-up time associated with any given session. In fact, there is very little that is predictable about a consultation, and this unpredictability can present departmental and managerial challenges. It can be difficult to balance librarians' workloads when researchers rarely schedule meetings as far in advance as committees and working groups do. Consequently, librarians face the task of guarding time for consultations from the pressures of rapidly filling calendars. Simply setting aside a day or two dedicated to consultations is rarely successful not only because researchers have questions and deadlines throughout the week, but also because a librarian can only conduct a limited number of effective consultations in one day. Because of this, the department head, library director, and anyone else with authority over consulting librarians should understand the mission, goals, and time commitment of this new service and support the consulting librarians' efforts.

In addition, developing this type of patron-centered service may influence the types of locations in which librarians work. Consultation programs aimed at students may thrive if offered in student centers or coffee shops. Faculty may appreciate librarians who spend time in their departments and laboratories. While the physical location of the library will certainly remain an important fixture on campus, library resources and services continue to move to the virtual realm as more and more users interact with the library remotely. This is especially true at institutions with non-residential students, distance learning programs, and faculty engaged in research that takes them off campus or even out of the country. Librarians should be prepared to keep abreast of where and when their patrons conduct research and should then structure and re-structure their consulting models to accommodate researchers' needs thus marrying the concepts of the field librarian and the consulting librarian. Additionally, librarians who are already "in the field" may meet new researchers who might not otherwise have sought assistance (M. Schnirring, phone conversation with author, May 9, 2007). In this way, consulting programs can help move the library and its resources beyond the library walls.

The personalization of services and resources is a trend in libraries that shows no sign of abating and is, in fact, essential for keeping libraries relevant and useful today. In this environment, research consultations fit well with an ethic of personalization both by providing personalized research help and by making use of other new personalized services. Increasingly, research sources will likely come from outside the physical library, and library research will likely be done from wherever the researcher may be at the moment. But the need for help navigating and managing scholarly literature is not likely to fade. As libraries work to reinvent and revitalize their services for the next generation of academic research, consultation programs can help to set the individual researcher at the center of the library's reference services. Not only do consultations alleviate the barriers that prevent researchers from receiving assistance, they also offer opportunities for tailored, one-on-one research support. Attending to the research needs of students, faculty, and administrators, and doing so in a manner that matches evolving research trends and resonates with each particular campus culture, increases the library's relevance on campus and the sense of trust between librarians and researchers. This in turn increases the researchers' willingness to seek further assistance knowing that they have a trusted ally in the library.

Acknowledgements

We are indebted to our colleagues in the Reference and Instruction department here at

Carleton College: Matt Bailey, Kristin Partlo, Charles Priore, Carolyn Sanford, and Heather Tompkins. They have all given generously of their time and wisdom.

We are also grateful to the librarians from other colleges and universities who took the time to tell us about their experiences: Ramona Islam (Senior Reference Librarian & Instruction Coordinator, Fairfield University), Lori Lampert (Reference Librarian, SUNY Brockport), Megan Lowe (Reference Librarian/Assistant Professor, University of Louisiana at Monroe), Caroline Reed (Reference Librarian, Jane Bancroft Cook Library, New College of Florida and University of South Florida Sarasota-Manatee), Marsha Schnirring (Instructional Services Librarian, Occidental College), and Loretta Ulincy (Public Services Librarian, DeSales University).

Sources for Additional Research

Cardwell, C., K. Furlong, and J. O'Keeffe. 2001. My librarian: Personalized research clinics and the academic library. *Research Strategies* 18 (2): 97-111.
>This article explores research consultation services at three different institutions. The scheduling, publicity, and evaluation decisions for each institution are explored.

Donham, J., and C. Williams Green. 2004. Developing a culture of collaboration: Librarian as consultant. *Journal of Academic Librarianship* 30 (4): 314-321.
>Cornell College librarians reorganized in order to foster more collaboration between themselves, the faculty, and students. They took on the title "Consulting Librarian" to help move from a model of knowledge transfer to one of student-centered knowledge. The addition of consultations as a service was a large, successful component. This article looks at how consultations can be a component of a larger collaborative service model.

Elmborg, J. K. 2002. Teaching at the desk: Toward a reference pedagogy. *portal: Libraries and the Academy* 2 (3): 455-464.
>Elmborg argues that reference interactions are a kind of teaching that must be varied to match student needs. While this article focuses on having a student-centered pedagogy at the reference desk, it is easy to see how the strategies outlined can and should be applied to research consultations.

Frank, D. G, G. K Raschke, J. Wood, and J. Z. Yang. 2001. Information consulting: The key to success in academic libraries. *The Journal of Academic Librarianship* 27 (2): 90-96.
>The authors see information consulting as an essential way for libraries to remain relevant on academic campuses. They take a broader view of information consulting to include all collaboration with scholars on research and teaching. Still, the focus remains on providing customized services to the academy in order to develop trust and to create opportunities.

Lee, D. 2004. Research consultations: Enhancing library research skills. *Reference Librarian* 41 (85): 169-180.
>Lee analyzes statistics from research consultations done at Mississippi State University to determine the marketing strategies that worked best for the different clientele that were targeted.

Whitson, W. 1995. Differentiated service: A new reference model. *Journal of Academic Librarianship* 21 (2): 103-110.

Whitson recommends breaking reference service into five distinct services with different staff, evaluations, and goals. Research consultation services are offered as the mechanism for providing research help to students. This paper outlines a scenario for setting up consultations as a part of a differentiated reference service model.

Yi, H. 2003. Individual research consultation service: An important part of an information literacy program. *Reference Services Review* 31 (4): 342-350.

Yi looks at consultations as an important part of the information literacy program and puts the consultations into an information literacy context. The author discusses the importance of integrating consultations into an information literacy program to complement instruction sessions.

Works Cited

Beck, S., and N. B. Turner. 2001. On the fly BI: Reaching and teaching from the reference desk. *The Reference Librarian* 34 (72): 83-96.

Cardwell, C., K. Furlong, and J. O'Keeffe. 2001. My librarian: Personalized research clinics and the academic library. *Research Strategies* 18 (2): 97-111.

Casey, M. E., and L. C. Savastinuk. 2006. Library 2.0. *Library Journal* 131 (14): 40-42.

Dodsworth, E. 1998. Marketing academic libraries: A necessary plan. *Journal of Academic Librarianship* 24 (4): 320-322.

Donham, J., and C. W. Green. 2004. Developing a culture of collaboration: Librarian as consultant. *Journal of Academic Librarianship* 30 (4): 314-321.

Elmborg, J. K. 2002. Teaching at the desk: Toward a reference pedagogy. *portal: Libraries and the Academy* 2 (3): 455-464.

Fox, A. 1998. Reference is BI. *OLA Quarterly* 4 (3): 6-7.

Frank, D. G., G. K. Raschke, J. Wood, and J. Z. Yang. 2001. Information consulting: The key to success in academic libraries. *The Journal of Academic Librarianship* 27 (2): 90-96.

Hughes, P., and A. Flandreau. 1980. Tutorial library instruction: The freshman program at Berea College. *Journal of Academic Librarianship* 6 (2): 91-94.

Simmons, M. Holschuh. 2005. Librarians as disciplinary discourse mediators: Using genre theory to move toward critical information literacy. *portal: Libraries and the Academy* 5 (3): 297-311.

Sonntag, G., and F. Palsson. 2007. No longer the sacred cow—no longer a desk: Transforming reference service to meet 21st century user needs. *Library Philosophy and Practice* (February). http://www.webpages.uidaho.edu/~mbolin/sonntag-palsson.htm.

Stalker, J. C., and M. E. Murfin. 1996. Quality reference service: A preliminary case study. *Journal of Academic Librarianship* 22 (6): 423-428.

Tyckoson, D. 2003. On the desirableness of personal relations between librarians and readers: The past and future of reference services. *Reference Services Review* 31 (1): 12-16.

Warnement, M. 2003. Size matters: The debate over reference desk height. *portal: Libraries and the Academy* 3 (1): 79-87.

Whitlatch, J. B. 2003. Reference futures: Outsourcing, the Web, or knowledge counseling. *Reference Services Review* 31 (1): 26-30.

Whitson, W. 1995. Differentiated service: A new reference model. *Journal of Academic Librarianship* 21 (2): 103-110.

Yi, H. 2003. Individual research consultation service: An important part of an information literacy program. *Reference Services Review* 31 (4): 342-350.

Notes

1. Of these, we communicated at length with librarians who responded from Occidental College, Fairfield University, SUNY Brockport, University of Louisiana at Monroe, DeSales University, and the joint program from New College of Florida and University of South Florida Sarasota-Manatee.

2. At New College of Florida and the University of South Florida Sarasota-Manatee, incoming freshmen are assigned a personal librarian just as they are assigned an academic advisor (C. Reed, phone conversation with author, May 3, 2007).

3. Occidental College in Los Angeles allows students the choice of scheduling a consultation with any available consulting librarian, regardless of subject, or with a librarian of their choice. This gives students the opportunity to choose the scheduling option that best fits their needs. This not only contributes to the sustainability of the model and gives librarians greater control over their schedules, but it also helps librarians broaden their skills in diverse research areas. (M. Schnirring, phone conversation with author, May 9, 2007).

4. The major drawback of this system is that it can seem impersonal to researchers if they feel they are making an appointment with an institution rather than with an individual. For this reason, libraries that choose this method of scheduling must work hard to emphasize the individualized help that is available via consultations.

5. When asked how they publicize their services, the consulting librarians we interviewed overwhelmingly identified these two strategies as key to their publicity programs.

6. At the end of each semester, librarians at the University of South Florida Sarasota-Manatee survey each student who participated in their My Librarian consultation program (C. Reed, phone conversation with author, May 3, 2007). The other assessment ideas surfaced from discussions within our own department here at Carleton and from Marsha Schnirring, who is interested in tracking the impact consultations have on student performances within individual classes at Occidental College (M. Schnirring, phone conversation with author, May 9, 2007).

CHAPTER 3

Reaching Beyond the Walls of the Library

Brenda L. Johnson and Laurie A. Alexander

Reference service matters—it matters today—and it will matter tomorrow. The abundance of information from Google, Elsevier, and others provides large aggregates of content that are directly accessible to scholars everywhere; in fact, the aggregators are often the first place users go for their research. As more users access these rich library collections in a variety of ways and new patterns of learning emerge, the demand for library services continues to increase. This shift transforms the way we think about providing reference and the role *place* plays in this interaction. Libraries have traditionally been places where knowledgeable assistance is provided and experts deliver high-level services. What would happen if the librarians were moved from one place—the library—to another—the department in which they serve? This chapter explores the relationship of the subject specialist to the concept of place through the field librarian model. Unlike traditional librarians, field librarians provide services within their academic departments, rather than inside the library itself. By investigating this innovative approach to reference services and exploring how services are responding to the needs of contemporary users, we will examine how the concept of a field librarian transforms reference services and the role of the subject specialist.

Next Generation of Reference Services

As we think about the next generation of reference services, we must acknowledge the importance of thinking creatively, the need to test our assumptions, and the importance of using a transformative process. It is not that we are at point X and need to get to point Y. Rather, we are setting new directions that prompt us to explore what we can do differently today to improve our services and take us in a better direction for tomorrow. By engaging in this manner, we acknowledge up front that we will take risks and create experiments to learn, and through that process discover what works and what does not. In fact, we may find that many of these ideas will need to go through several iterations before they work well.

Across the country, libraries are creating new services to better meet changing campus needs. Reference departments provide virtual reference and engage faculty and students via online chat and other tools. Curriculum integration initiatives are focused on deploying programmatic and technology resources. The result of these efforts is that more of the library's digital resources and services are integrated into campus course management systems. Yet, despite significant strides, it is important to recognize that we need to continue developing new initiatives, engaging in new activities to remain relevant, and doing so in ways that are concrete rather than abstract. We need to dramatically challenge our traditional notions of subject specialists, their roles, and their relationship to the library as a place.

Innovative Outreach

John Seeley Brown, the Former Chief Scientist of Xerox Corporation and Director of its Palo Alto Research Center (PARC), has spoken a great deal about the power of social learning and the need for higher education to tap into the growing phenomenon of the blending of cognitive and social activities. He states that "many kids today do more than just explore the Web: they create, tinker, share and build on each others' creations. We are slowly reconstructing a culture of tinkering, which lays the foundation for a grounded understanding of theoretical topics that you learn about in school" (Neal 2007). He further suggests that as we understand more about how people learn and the evolving role of technology, our approach to services also changes. As Brown has asserted in several public presentations, reference librarians have become the guides and mentors for productive inquiry. This philosophy provides a remarkable framework for thinking about ways to develop and deploy outreach efforts.

Ubiquitous access has significant implications for the ways that libraries are staffed. Some traditional library tasks will go away, others will be consolidated, and still others will morph into something new. What do these changes mean for reference services and, specifically, for subject specialists and their roles? The role of the subject specialist includes liaison duties and outreach work with academic departments, collection development, research consultation, and course-integrated instruction. Over the past several years, librarians have placed significant importance on outreach. We have been actively engaged in exploring the relationship among programmatic services, spaces (both physical and virtual) that foster collaboration and enrichment of the academic experience, access to information, and emergent information technologies. The role of the subject specialist has become more complex and more fully integrated into scholarship, teaching, and learning. This change has translated into a range of activities, including strengthening existing services, building new ones, and updating facilities.

Librarians are and will be working with users in their environment, whether in person, by e-mail, in chat rooms, or through other technological mechanisms not yet identified. There is growing demand to provide services in non-library facilities. The traditional approach to outreach has changed dramatically over the past few years and we expect that this trend will continue. Faculty and students are interacting with librarians in new ways. We must continue to be even more aggressive about providing a diverse set of options for users and interacting with them in their communities. One such effort to work outside of the library walls is the University of Michigan field librarian program.

Transforming Reference and the Field Librarian Program

By using the University of Michigan's field librarian program as an example, we can begin to explore how libraries can transform their reference services. A few years ago, the University of Michigan Library partnered with the School of Art & Design, the Women's Studies Program, and the Department of Classical Studies to pilot the concept of a field librarian. The original intent of this program was to develop a new approach to the role of subject specialists by focusing on the librarian's role as an integrated research partner. The premise was that the field librarian would have office space and spend a large portion of his or her time in the department instead of residing in a traditional library building. With financial support from the Provost's Office, the Library recruited three field librarians, one for each of the three academic units. The concept quickly moved from pilot to ongoing service.

Moving the Field Librarian Concept to a Program

The original proposal for the field librarian program includes on-site consultation, support for instructional technology, and research support for faculty and graduate students in their departments. This program offers a compromise between one-on-one support and generalized services, and also places the subject-specialist librarian in the setting most likely to promote active engagement with faculty, graduate students, and departments. This program focuses support services on the continuum of individual faculty needs in the specific context of their disciplines. Potential assignments are identified by working closely with schools, colleges, and departments to determine areas with the most potential for active partnership.

Sample Discipline-Specific Proposal: Art & Design Field Librarian

The University Library is proposing to fund a permanent librarian position whose office would be located in the School of Art and Design and who would work directly with faculty and students of the School. The Librarian would be responsible for Media Union Library collection development in the area of art and design, would provide studio and research consultation, orientations, course-integrated instruction and workshops designed to foster the innovative use of traditional and non-traditional library resources. Working with faculty, the Librarian will support effective applications of new technologies for teaching and learning. The Librarian will also supervise an additional position that will be responsible for capturing the creative process on video and film.

Examples of additional kinds of support the Librarian might provide, based on the needs of the School include:

- Conducting screenings of art videos for students
- Identifying digital art content and design of systems to facilitate access
- Assisting in planning and implementing small or large-scale digitization projects of appropriate resources.

Since the benefit of the field librarian model depends upon the successful integration of the librarian's expertise within the research and teaching activities of the department, flexibility in position responsibilities is an important component at the outset.

As a librarian appointment within the University Library, the field librarian will participate in the full range of professional activities. This might include serving on library committees and task forces, providing reference service, collaborating with colleagues on special projects and initiatives, participating in long-term planning and service assessment, and attending meetings as appropriate.

The Library will conduct a national search for a highly qualified individual, and the successful candidate will be expected to bring a complement of advanced subject knowledge of studio art and design, educational technology expertise, and an appreciation for the creative process. Faculty and students would have the opportunity to participate in the search process and provide input on the candidate selection.

The Library pledged to provide a full-time, permanent position with salary commensurate with the librarian rank, an administrative "home" for the position, mentoring, performance evaluation, ongoing professional development opportunities, and general support (i.e. computer, technical support, etc). The departments and schools agreed to provide office space and welcome the field librarian as a colleague within the department.

The key to moving field librarianship from a concept to a program is to engage a key grouping of departments in an early pilot. Since the original three departments partnered with us, several others have approached us about a field librarian for their area. For example, one of the Deans heard so many positive things about the School of Art and Design field librarian that he wanted to know why his school did not have one. Similarly, at a national conference a few years ago, the chair of the Classical Studies department spoke proudly about his field librarian, which led the chair at a prominent university to ask why he did not have one. What did this tell us? By shifting our thinking about subject specialists and the relationship to place, we became relevant in new and exciting ways.

⊠ *a*⊠*ing a* ⊠*ie*⊠*l Li*⊠*rarian* ⊠*rogram* ⊠*ecome a* ⊠*ea*⊠*it*⊠

Since the inception of the program, the field librarians have had job descriptions that included components that were similar to other subject specialists, such as providing reference services, selecting materials for the collection, and engaging in instructional activities. The position proposals were our best guess at the time about what the field librarian might do.

Within months of each Field Librarian being hired, they were able to articulate their role uniquely within the context of their discipline, departmental culture, politics, and academic directions. Their ability to do so was directly linked to their *immersion* in the department. The following was critical to their success: participation of each department in hiring the Field Librarian, their physical location in the academic unit, and the early work of each Field Librarian in shaping their role. The result was an environment where the Field Librarian was viewed as a colleague, rather than an external liaison. Over time, these position descriptions evolved and broadened in positive ways that were not conceived or anticipated at the beginning of this initiative. (Johnson and Alexander 2007, 40)

All subject specialists are involved in collection development, and field librarians are no exception. However, because of their close working relationship with faculty members, they have a broader and deeper knowledge of current research needs. This understanding has encouraged a deeper level of engagement between the faculty members and the field librarians. For example, Beau Case, the Classical Studies field librarian, was able to intercede when a graduate student had planned to travel to Europe to use Greek manuscripts essential to his dissertation. Instead, Beau was able to purchase microfilm or digital copies of these manuscripts. The student was not planning to ask Beau for assistance in locating these materials; rather it was a casual conversation about another matter that alerted Beau to the graduate student's research needs. This conversation probably would not have happened had Beau been sitting in the library. In addition, faculty members are becoming more engaged in the acquisition of materials for the library. For example, Beau coached archaeologists on how to obtain rare materials for the library collection as they were traveling around the world visiting various excavation sites.

The field librarians have been able to create special partnerships with their faculty. Annette Haines, the Art & Design field librarian, describes it by saying:

Artists know to turn to a librarian for help in finding a book, but few artists would consider asking a librarian to help find materials for art projects. As the Art & Design Field Librarian, I am immersed in student and faculty life and have a unique opportunity to educate artists about the librarian as a resource for a wide variety of information. My outreach to artists new to campus, both faculty and students, begins early and most of my initial conversations focus on the kinds of questions they should feel free to ask me. During orientations and library instruction sessions, I like to emphasize that I embrace the artist's unusual questions and see it as one of the most enjoyable parts of my job. (Johnson and Alexander 2007, 30)

Students and faculty have incorporated her philosophy. For example, a student asked Annette to help him find samples of chitosan, the structural element in insect exoskeletons. Annette, using her research skills, successfully obtained the information needed to locate this unusual material for his art project.

Field librarians are also heavily involved with instruction. Amy Robb, the former Women's Studies field librarian, was instrumental in developing a new approach to course integrated instruction. This approach resulted in faculty recognizing a significant improvement in the quality of student research and written papers. Her close work with faculty on this initiative resulted in the restructuring of assignments to include more meaningful use of library resources. Similarly, Beau was able to take a different approach to incorporating library instruction within the Classical Studies curriculum. He redesigned a standing subject course, meant to introduce first year graduate students to classical studies, to include key research strategies and resources. The graduate students were able to transfer the skills learned in this course to their work in other courses.

As the departments began to realize the value of field librarians, their support for this program increased. For example, they have provided substantial travel support for book buying trips and professional domain-specific conferences for the librarian. They have given the field librarians faculty appointments, assigned them to curriculum committees, and have enhanced their offices and work spaces.

Importance of Proximity

The proximity between field librarians and scholars forms a new relationship that transforms the scholarly workflow. In essence, their immersion has enabled them to become active partners in the scholarly process.

> The presence of the Field Librarians in the department made them accessible and greatly enhanced lines of communication with faculty. In the natural course of bumping into faculty in the hall, relationships were informally formed that ultimately developed into new collegial patterns. These librarians were no longer viewed as collection bound, rather as resources and active partners in the department. (Johnson and Alexander 2007, 40)

A great deal has been written about the effect of proximity on work performance. The literature covers a range of topics related to the impact of proximity, from time of day, to duration of interaction, to the proliferation of technology. Why is physical proximity so important? In a report on telecommuting, John Niles focuses on the question of physical proximity in the workplace and reports the following.

> Physical proximity of workers in an office usually yields a high level of casual, serendipitous, spontaneous, nonintrusive communication among office staff. Communications between people who are nearby can be more easily synchronized to times when all parties are mentally ready to focus on the communications…Staff located in separate places must be much more intentional in their efforts to communicate. (Niles 1994)

Put another way, "proximity is the probability of people being in the same 'communication location' during the same interval of time" (Monge 1980, 112).

The value of chance and impromptu interactions cannot be ignored. There has been much research about the effect proximity in the workplace has on creating an environment of commitment and trust. When colleagues are in face-to-face situations,

> [P]eople instinctively attend to the other people around them, assessing body language, attitude, and other visual and verbal clues to determine credibility. Proximity to colleagues provides security, generates atmosphere and fosters collaboration and discussion… Proximity to colleagues also allows for quick access to implicit knowledge and extended personal networks and promotes an awareness of projects around which allows knowledge sharing despite not being directly involved. (Yuhua 2004, 15-16)

Despite the importance of proximity, the success of the field librarian program cannot be entirely attributed to the physical location of the librarian. Librarians in charge of departmental libraries are located near and have frequent contact with faculty and students. What distinguishes the field librarian from the departmental librarian? For one thing, directors of departmental libraries have many administrative duties. They must keep the library doors open, hire and train staff, deal with a myriad of facilities issues, develop and maintain the collection and many other managerial duties. The time that they have to interact with faculty and students is therefore more limited than the time that field librarians have. Another difference is that departmental librarians are in the "field" but their field is the *library*. The field librarian's "field" is the *academic department* with which they are affiliated. This distinction in location may at first glance seem trivial, however, we believe it makes a very large difference in the communication that takes place.

As faculty and students walk through the doors into a departmental library, the nature of their communication changes. Their encounters with librarians are more purposeful, and the communication is more formal. When a librarian's office is located in the library, he/she tends to be associated with the collection and a set of rules and policies wrapped around the use of that collection and that physical space. This association changes when the librarian's office is located in the department, which enables a faculty member to pop his/her head into the field librarian's office. A very different dynamic develops (or exists) when a faculty member runs into a field librarian while sipping coffee in the lounge rather than in the formal setting of a library. This shared and familiar environment creates an atmosphere of comfort and builds the foundation for a solid working relationship. Furthermore, the field librarians have capitalized on the importance of proximity to develop these types of connections. Perhaps even more than originally anticipated, the field librarians have built strong partnerships with faculty by embedding themselves into their communities and thereby, the scholarly activities of the faculty.

The Future of the Field Librarian Program
To date, the assessment of the field librarian program has been admittedly informal.

Yet, opinions shared shed light on the program. Faculty and students are effusive in their praise and recognition of the importance and value of the field librarians. As mentioned earlier, deans and department chairs speak with great pride about "their" field librarians, and the program has even been a topic of discussion at national conferences.

Annette Haines was among twenty-three faculty and staff members recognized at the University of Michigan for their teaching, scholarship, service, and creative activities. She was nominated by a faculty member in the School of Art and Design and the written nomination demonstrated both an appreciation for Annette's achievements and her role as a field librarian. The University faculty and staff newspaper reported,

> When Haines arrived in 2002 the school was in the early stages of a curricular overhaul. The school also had to keep pace with changes in the ways faculty are required to structure and present teaching materials. She was invaluable in augmenting the library's collections in several areas, and in offering workshops to assist faculty working with a wide range of equipment, materials and technologies. She has done everything possible, colleagues say, to invite, inspire, lead, teach and simply be available when students, staff and faculty request her assistance. (University Record 2006)

Why is this example important? It is important because the award signifies that the field librarian program has moved from a concept to a valued and mainstream service. The services of the library are being recognized in direct connection with the mission of research and teaching.

A common complaint among academic librarians is that we are not effective at getting the word out about all the good and innovative things we are doing. Despite our best efforts, most faculty and students know little about the services that libraries offer. The field librarian program, without our implicit intention, has become a powerful public relations tool. It has become an effective way of communicating and informing our constituents about what we are doing and can do for them.

Programs, such as field librarianship, bring together partners and create an unexpected and positive learning experience that prompts us to think more dynamically about the way library services are conceived and delivered. The field librarian program has been a success. As we think about expansion and scalability, we do not want to lose what makes this program so effective. Although we can and have moved towards librarians working outside the libraries, taking on many of the attributes of a field librarian, we firmly believe that it is not enough to simply change the name of a subject specialist to a field librarian. In order for future field librarians to succeed, they must have all of the opportunities afforded by the framework of this program. Further expansion requires funding from interested schools/departments and the University administration. These are key factors for any library thinking about deploying a field librarian program.

Library Outreach Services

Although we are most familiar with the field librarian program, a review of the literature demonstrates there are many libraries actively transforming their outreach services. Below are a number of examples.

Rovin' Reference at Occidental College

This example demonstrates how an idea from one institution can trigger the development of a new service at another institution. Marsha Schnirring, Instructional Services Librarian at Occidental College, learned about a public librarian in London who provided Sunday reference on street corners. Intrigued by this idea, she started looking for opportunities to incorporate this concept at her own institution, so when the first year experience program was looking for ways to incorporate services into their living and learning communities, she presented the idea of Rovin' Reference. One hour a day, four days a week, the librarians provide face-to-face reference services to first year students in their residence hall. In an e-mail conversation with the authors on May 16, 2007, Schnirring shared one of her favorite examples of the success of this program—the time that several students lined up for help and a spontaneous collaborative group research session resulted. The popularity of the program has resulted in the inclusion of Rovin' Reference in the new first year student housing building that is being planned.

Librarian With a Latte at the University of Michigan

Eric Frierson, a librarian at the University of Michigan, uses a variety of tools to provide reference. Examples include traditional methods (such as the reference desk) and virtual methods (such as instant messaging, e-mail, blogs, and *Facebook*). Most recently, Frierson has been going to a local coffee shop with his laptop and inviting students to stop by for assistance. Why a coffee shop? A coffee shop is where the students are already working. Frierson goes on to share that "going to where students are seems to be a theme in social-networking discussions, and they mean virtually. … It's equally important to go where they are physically" (Carlson 2007). Frierson highlights the importance of place and face-to-face interaction time. He states, "an interaction that would take half an hour online takes five minutes in person" (Carlson 2007).

Mobile Librarian at University of Notre Dame

This example demonstrates how learning theory can inform practice and the importance of being willing to try out new ideas. Leslie Morgan, Librarian in Residence at the University of Notre Dame, was instrumental in launching a Mobile Librarian service. In an e-mail conversation with the authors on May 23, 2007, Morgan wrote that the "millennial student wants the quickest and least path of resistance to information." By taking the library on the road, the librarians have been better able to provide reference, instructional sessions, faculty consultations, and promotion of the services. Instead of sitting at the reference desk, the librarian goes to a student focal point such as a residence hall or the student services building. While there is no formal assessment in place to test this model, the interactions with students demonstrate that there is a need for this type of service and that it is being used. Future plans for this project include adding colleagues and increasing the locations and hours of the service.

Mobile Teaching at California State University Monterey Bay

Reference librarians at California State University Monterey Bay have offered a series of drop-in reference and instructional sessions with a twist: "they, rather than the students, will be the ones dropping in" (Baker 2007). Wireless access has enabled librarians to reach out to users in popular gathering places such as residence halls, the Black Box Cabaret (an eating, lounging and performance space), and the University Center. In these settings, the librarians provide reference and research assistance—from articulation of the information needed, to source identification, to search strategies, to information analysis. At the end of the sessions, the students are asked to complete a Web-based survey about the service. This in turn, assists in the ongoing development of the service.

Direct-to-You Reference at the University of Texas at San Antonio

This program embraces the importance of piloting ideas and taking chances. The librarians at the University of Texas at San Antonio embarked on a pilot project to provide reference service at the writing center, the tutoring center, the computer lab, and the residence halls. By taking the "let's try it and see what happens approach," they were able to expand their services to students. They are currently developing an assessment tool and marketing strategies (Chapman).

My Librarian Program at New College and the University of South Florida, Sarasota

A decrease in library usage recently prompted the New College and University of South Florida Sarasota-Manatee libraries to join forces and develop services that better meet the needs of users. Together, they were able to innovate and think creatively about how to reach beyond the walls of the library. "Group orientations were abandoned in favor of one-on-one tours, letters and e-mails sent individually to students replaced campus-wide announcements, and follow up surveys were introduced to measure student satisfaction. The result has been a nearly 500% increase in students' use of the library over the past year" (New College 2007). They attribute the success of the program to the personal contact of an individualized service.

Curtin University of Technology: Library and Information Services (LIS) Model

The final example focuses on the importance of proximity of users and service. Librarians at Curtin University of Technology (formerly the West Australian Institute of Technology) have deployed a new service called Library and Information Services (LIS). The LIS focuses on the specific needs of researchers. Five senior librarians work closely with the researchers in their divisions. They observed that "the most radical part of the new model was to place the Senior Librarians outside the library building. They would each have an office in their respective divisions and become a critical part of the teaching, learning, and research life within those divisions" (Vautier 2001, 93). By embedding the librarians in the communities they serve, they are more in-tune with their users and better able to provide timely and relevant reference. The collaboration between researcher and librarian occurred as a result of proximity.

Beyond the Walls of the Library

Outreach efforts are important in the age of ubiquitous access. Users have a vast array of skills, needs, and expectations; the challenge is to reshape our reference services to reflect the way that they think and work. In order to reach this goal, we must strengthen our connections with faculty and students. We must expand outreach services by finding new ways to bring the resources and expertise of the library to the university community and beyond. We must also educate the campus community by firmly establishing the library in the minds of our users as a rich information environment, an ever-ready source of help in navigating that environment, and a potential partner in curriculum development and research.

We are living in an information rich world that enables information to be sought anytime, anywhere. Peter Morville says, "ambient findability describes a fast emerging world where we can find anyone or anything from anywhere at any time. We're not there yet, but we're headed in the right direction. Information is in the air, literally" (Morville 2005, 6). In this highly digitized and networked environment, the question of findability becomes a critical concept, and therefore, the role of reference services becomes even more essential.

The library has a long and distinguished tradition of providing rich and relevant services for users. Whether helping a patron with research, teaching new resources to an introductory class, providing virtual reference assistance, or delivering documents to user desktops, the mission of the library is to connect users with the information they are seeking. Geoffrey Freeman, an architect specializing in libraries, states, "[r]ather than threatening the traditional concept of the library, the integration of new information technology has actually become the catalyst that transforms the library into a more vital and critical intellectual center of life at colleges and universities today" (CLIR 2005). Libraries are about collections, but they are also about providing much more. We must provide a unique learning environment where traditional resources, emerging information technologies, and a user-focused suite of services bring together researchers and learners from various disciplines. This environment will sometimes be in a library building, and other times not. It is important to engage in experimentation to reach this goal by expanding our notion of place and reaching out to users. This is the future of library services.

Sources for Additional Research

Council on Library and Information Resources. 2005. *Library as place rethinking roles, rethinking space.* Washington, DC: Council on library and information resources. http://www.clir.org/pubs/reports/pub129/pub129.pdf.
> Librarians, architects, and professors explore a number of questions related to technology, library space, and the relationship between the two. The chapter by Geoffrey Freeman delves into the changing views of libraries and how the library is seen as an extension of the academic experience.

Johnson, B. J. and L. A. Alexander. 2007. In the field: An innovative role puts academic librarians right in the department they serve. *Library Journal* 132 (2): 38-40.
> This publication explores the Field Librarian Program (FLP) offered by the University of Michigan Library. The FLP has transformed the role of the subject specialist and has encouraged us to move more deliberately toward perpetuating this model across the organization.

Morville, P. 2005. *Ambient Findability.* Sebastopol, CA: O'Reilly.
> This publication describes the future of information and connectivity, examining how the melding of innovations like GIS and the Internet will impact the global marketplace and society at large in the 21st century.

Neal, L. Five Questions… for John Seeley Brown. http://www.elearnmag.org/subpage.cfm?section=articles&article=37-1.
> An interview with John Seeley Brown, chief scientist of Xerox Corporation and the director of its Palo Alto Research Center (PARC) explores the Web as transformative medium and technology innovations as they relate to learning.

Oblinger, D. 2006. *Learning spaces.* Boulder: EDUCAUSE.
> This book explores learner expectations as they relate to place and how libraries can create learning environments for a variety of users. By outlining the principles and activities of learning and relating them to issues raised by emerging information technologies, the authors are able to provide a framework for thinking about libraries and the spaces (both virtual and physical) where learning occurs.

Seamans, N. H. and P. Metz. 2002. Virginia Tech's Innovative College Librarian Program. *College & Research Libraries* 63 (4): 324-332.
> This article discusses the formation of a College Librarian Program. The early history of the program is described and an overall analysis is given describing the benefits of moving towards this model of reference.

Weber, L. and R. Britton. 2000. Academic Library Information Centers: A New Service Approach for Subject Support. *Behavior and Social Sciences Librarian* 19: 53-60.
> This article explores the relationship between collections and subject specialists. The University of Southern California closed the Education and the Social Work branch libraries in August and the process for developing a new reference service model without direct access to a paper collection is described.

Works Cited

Baker, P. and J. Silveria. Taking it to the Streets: The Mobile Librarian at CSUMB.

http://wetec.csumb.edu/site/x17626.xml.

Carlson, S. 2007. Are reference desks dying out? *Chronicle of Higher Education* 53 (33): A37-A39.

Chapman, K. and D. D. Bosque. Chucking chat: Going to where our students REALLY are. http://data.webjunction.org/wj/documents/12560.pdf.

Council on Library and Information Resources (CLIR). 2005. *Library as place rethinking roles, rethinking space*. Washington, DC: Council on library and information resources. http://www.clir.org/pubs/reports/pub129/pub129.pdf.

Johnson, B.J. and L. A. Alexander. 2007. In the field: An innovative role puts academic librarians right in the department they serve. *Library Journal* 132 (2): 38-40.

Morville, P. 2005. *Ambient findability*. Sebastopol, CA: O'Reilly.

Monge, P. R. and K. K Kirste. 1980. Measuring proximity in human organization. *Social Psychology Quarterly* 43 (1): 110-115.

Neal, L. Five Questions...for John Seeley Brown. http://www.elearnmag.org/subpage.cfm?section=articles&article=37-1.

New College, USF Library Project Showcased at National Conference. http://www.ncf.edu/PublicAffairs/documents/Librarians.htm.

Niles, J. 1994. Beyond telecommuting: A new paradigm for the effect of telecommunications on travel. http://www.lbl.gov/ITSD/Niles/.

University Record. 2006. *Annual awards fete top faculty. http://www.umich.edu/~urecord/0607/Oct02_06/02.shtml.*

Vautier, L., J. Hanlon, and G. Jones. "Senior librarians as partners in research: The Curtin experience." In *Changing roles for Australian Technology Network Libraries,* ed. John Frylinck. Adelaide: University of South Australia Library, 2001.

Yuhua L., ed. 2004. *Cooperative design, visualization, and engineering: First international conference, CDVE 2004, Palma de Mallorca, Spain, September 19-22, 2004, Proceedings*. New York: Springer.

CHAPTER 4

Solution Focused Reference: Counselor Librarianship Revisited

Ross T. LaBaugh

Oprah is born. FORTRAN runs. Ike signs the new Federal Highway Act. Michigan opens the nation's first shopping mall. IBM begins selling computers. *The Lord of the Rings* (the book) is a hit. It is 1954.

A half a century later, Oprah is God. FORTRAN is still running. The Federal Highway Administration has a budget of over thirty-four billion dollars. The Mall of America is one of the most popular tourist destinations in the United States. IBM is the largest information technology company on the planet. *The Lord of the Rings* (the movie) is a hit.

Who would have thought?

To most in the library world, 1954 was pretty ordinary. L. Quincy Mumford was named Librarian of Congress. The American Library Association countered McCarthyism with the *Freedom to Read* manifesto. Reference service zigged when it should have zagged.

Let me explain. In March 1954, David K. Maxfield, a librarian and professor, published a report on a program at the University of Illinois, Chicago (UIC), then a small college on Navy Pier, which could have changed the direction of reference service forever. In a little circulated document called *Counselor Librarianship: A New Departure*, Maxfield (1954a) described how the UIC used four seemingly separate streams (general education, library instruction, reference services, and student counseling) to re-vision the traditional approach to reference services and create a confluence called "Counselor Librarianship."

While the program itself was short-lived, the impact that it could have had, and still may have, on our profession cannot be overstated. In the next few pages, I would like to explain a bit more about the Counselor Librarian approach, and suggest how using a therapeutic technique called Solution Focused Therapy (SFT) might be a way to rekindle some of Maxfield's notions and realign reference service to its intended roots.

By 1954, the surge of soldiers back from WWII had given way to a more predictable student population of recent high school graduates ready for higher education. Now, instead of dealing with America's Greatest Generation, faculty, administrators, counselors, and librarians once again faced undergraduates who were much less mature and much more inexperienced, untested, and unsure. These new freshmen were kids. Concurrently, librarians, having weathered the GI onslaught, found that they could now focus less attention on the physical and technical aspects of the library, and concentrate more on "… questions on basic educational philosophy and long-time library objectives" (Maxfield 1954a, 3).

A few years prior, Harvard published what would become the founding document on general education, *General Education in a Free Society* (Harvard 1945), and many colleges, including UIC, were investigating ways to enable students to learn to think, communicate effectively, and "arouse a student's intellectual curiosity" (Maxfield 1954a, 4). This exploration inspired the librarians to "step-up" library instruction programs and redefine objectives. From the UIC Library's Annual Report for 1948/49 comes this objective:

> To suggest how the world of books and journals reflects, influences and is a part of all sciences, arts and professions, and how critically chosen and systematically used books and journals may broaden intellectual outlook, contribute toward the implementation of social and civic responsibility, increase efficiencies in practical affairs, enhance personality resources and sharpen the zest of living all life long. (University 1948-49, 8)

Masked by the quaintness of the rhetoric, there is an underlying hint of what we now call information literacy, community engagement, social responsibility, and life-long learning.

Up to this point, however, academic libraries had long defined good reference librarians as those who placed "...heaviest emphasis in their daily work on library materials, bibliographic techniques, and the literal, surface aspects of the particular problems presented to them from hour to hour" (Maxfield 1954a, 7). In their well known volume, *Rothstein on Reference*, Katz (1989, 235) and others point out that the focus of reference was clearly on the collection (e.g. Mudge's *Guide to Reference Books*), rather than the notion of the reference librarian as an active participant in student learning.

Finally, the UIC Counseling Bureau, facing this new generation of students, began utilizing the library for vocational materials, educational planning, and research on the newly developing field of "student personnel." In addition, psychological and psychiatric terms were filtering into the mainstream consciousness. Schools, businesses, social service agencies, and organizations of all sorts were realizing the importance of good mental health in all aspects of their operations. The Library and the Counseling Bureau likewise realized that they were addressing many of the same students and many of the same needs. Maxfield candidly remarked on the contemporary perspective of many librarians toward students, and revealed his more holistic approach.

> Their individual patrons, sentient and sensitive, at varying stages of development, sometimes well-informed subject experts, often ignorant and unable to read well, occasionally arrogant, not infrequently frightened, likely to be under some sort of pressure, and often baffled or frustrated, tend to register on them as impersonalized, uniform statistics. (Maxfield 1954a, 9)

With these four forces merging, UIC took the bold step of establishing a new breed of librarians "to help patrons change behavior and grow by listening to them; by encouraging them to understand their own feelings; and by helping clients define basic problems and establish strategies for dealing with those problems" (Lukenbill 1983, 83). With considerable effort at recruitment and significant training with the university's counselors, advisors, and psychologists, UIC renamed its traditional reference desk the Advisory Information Desk. This new desk was staffed with Counselor Librarians who not only assisted students with the traditional search for information to support their studies, but guided students to resources on self-understanding, personal growth, reading techniques, educational planning, and vocational information. (Maxfield 1954b, 164).

While this may seem radical for the time, Patrick Penland, in his piece from the *Encyclopedia of Library and Information Science,* traces the foundation for the Counselor Librarian back to the Roman Empire. He notes that the aristocracy placed great value on reading as a form of *intrapersonal* (emphasis mine) communication. Through reading came questioning, curiosity, reflection, self education, and improvement. Presumably, a librarian was selecting and organizing materials and guiding readers to them (Penland 1971 6: 241). Librarianship has always been a helping profession, the Counselor Librarian model was simply another way of helping.

The UIC Library must have been a remarkably forward-thinking place to design this model of service and then have the wherewithal to follow through with it. The reference department was abolished and additional Counselor Librarians were specially recruited, hired, and intensively trained in counseling and advisement. Under the tutelage of the Counseling Bureau, they studied aspects of student personnel, problem identification, learning process, group communication, psychology, and study skills. They participated in mock interviews and became fully immersed in the literature and practice of what we would now call student affairs. In a year's time, they were ready to implement their new model.

What exactly did these Counselor Librarians do? Since it was the 1950s, it is likely that they spent a good deal of time filing cards, ordering books and pamphlets, and managing the collection. They still answered reference questions, advised students on appropriate reading, and taught library instruction classes. Their uniqueness, however, lay not so much in what they did, but in their approach.

> [The] answering of reference questions and the provision of assistance toward the solution of bibliographic problems is now being done in a manner more commensurate with general education philosophy and student personnel methods. Thanks to the in-service training, greater interviewing finesse is possible... and more effective effort is also being made to encourage students to...think through their reference problems and formulate their questions.... (Maxfield 1954a, 24)

By all accounts, the Counselor Librarian approach was a success. Circulation increased, basic reference-type questions decreased, requests for library instruction rose, and students seemed to become more independent and thoughtful learners. According to Maxfield, by 1953,

> the shift in emphasis… has produced a new 'climate' of library activity. The response of the individual students to the more personalized service has been excellent and enthusiastic collaboration between student and librarian has been the order of the day. The emphasis on developmental matters and on 'heuristics,' has… gone far toward removing some of the possible limitation of the conventional approach for undergraduates. (Maxfield 1954a, 3)

A year later, *College and Research Libraries* published an article about the program at UIC (Maxfield 1954b) and then there is nothing more in the literature. Fifty years later, despite a flash of interest in the 1970s (Penland, Jennerich), the brilliance of the Counselor Librarian model has all but disappeared. In 1983, Lukenbill speculated that several factors may have contributed to the failure of the model: a return to a book-centered approach to library management; the lack of preparedness by librarians to accept a larger role in the social and emotional aspects of students' lives; the profession's resistance to include behavioral science as part of its knowledge base; and, the public's reluctance to consider librarians beyond their stereotypical and traditional image (Lukenbill 1983). While any or all of these factors may have been true at the time, the current environment may now be right to rekindle the ember of Maxfield's premise by shifting reference service from an academic model to a therapeutic one.

Before moving forward in the discussion of this paradigm shift, it is necessary to establish a baseline definition of counseling therapy and its practitioners, and to summarize several major approaches to treatment.

Counseling has been defined in many ways:

- "… the removal of perceptions and attitudes which tend to block thinking and learning" (Penland 1971, 240).
- "Counseling is an artistic endeavor that uses scientific methodology to help people lead more effective lives" (Weikel 2006, 61).
- "Counseling is a process that helps people learn about themselves, their environment, and ways to handle their roles and relationships" (Hansen 1977, ix).
- "Counseling is an intimate form of learning" (Corey 2004, 17).
- "Counseling is a process in which clients learn how to make decisions and formulate new ways of behaving, feeling, and thinking" (Brammer, et al. 1993, 27).

Furthermore, just as there is no shortage of definitions of counseling, there is no shortage of those who counsel (e.g. physicians, psychologists, rabbis, sheikhs). All have differing academic credentials and titles. From the client's perspective, the only thing that matters is that they are helpers.

In *Theory and Practice of Counseling and Psychotherapy*, Gerald Corey (2004) breaks counseling down into five categories.

Analytic (early twentieth century)

Freud's pioneering work on consciousness and its influence on development launched the notion of psychoanalytic therapy. Adler and Jung, while also believing in early formative personalities, focused their attention on their patients' present and future behaviors.

Experiential and Relationship-Oriented (mid-twentieth century)

Later, the existentialists (e.g. Frankl, May) and the Gestaltists (e.g. Perls) alleged that trauma in early life is no excuse for dysfunction ten, twenty, or fifty years later. While these and other similar models may vary in their approaches, they do share a common belief that the relationship between client and therapist is the key to success.

Action Therapies (mid- to late twentieth century)

By the mid-twentieth century, behavioral psychologists began emphasizing the cause and effect nature of human behavior. From Skinner's classical conditioning, Bandura and Beck's social and cognitive aspects, and Ellis' rational emotive therapy evolved an all encompassing belief that a modification of thoughts and beliefs (often through learning) can lead to behavioral change. Concurrently, Rogers chose a humanistic path toward understanding human behavior by concentrating on our capacity to heal ourselves. He and his followers espoused a nondirective, "person-centered," and empathetic approach to therapy. Maxfield and Penland often referred to Rogers in their work on therapeutic reference. As with all action therapies, the therapeutic relationship between client and therapist is seen as crucial.

Systems Perspective (late twentieth century)

In the late 1960s, some therapists, questioning the male, white dominated, hierarchical nature of their profession, branched out into new areas which recognized individuals as part of a larger social system, such as a family, organization, culture or community.

Postmodern/Present Approach

The basic premise of postmodernism is that our "reality" is what we make it, we express that "reality" through language and narrative, and our perspective on "reality" varies depending on those around us. In a postmodern world, this notion (often called social constructionism) alters both our view of a situation and our actions within a situation by taking into account all relevant variables. In other words, we see what we think we see. We believe what we want to believe. From a counseling perspective, a postmodern approach changes the focus of the therapeutic direction of the client from "what was" to "what is," and then facilitates intervention strategies to reach what "will be." The therapist abandons any authoritative position and instead becomes a "listener-facilitator" (Corey 2004, 387). This is an extremely pragmatic approach which, though not appropriate for complex conditions, clearly has its use in short term therapy.

I believe this postmodern model is where reference librarians need to focus their attention, for it is here, in the therapeutic relationship between librarian and client, that we can redefine "help" in a human, rather than a technological way. I also believe that Maxfield was simply ahead of his time. Had his Counselor Librarian approach been introduced in a postmodern world which embraced social constructionism instead of psychoanalysis, librarianship could have more easily aligned itself with social work and counseling rather than with computing, academia, and business. It is here, specifically in a type of cognitive behavioral therapy called Solution Focused Therapy (SFT), that reference belongs.

What Exactly is Solution-Focused Therapy (SFT)?

SFT, credited to Steve de Shazer and Insoo Kim Berg of the Brief Therapy Center in Milwaukee, found that people present themselves for counseling to solve one problem, and to solve it quickly. Not only do they not want long term, multiphase treatment, Berg discovered that, if promptly and strategically handled, short term therapy is actually more successful than prolonged counseling. Rather than spending hours and hours on the client's early experiences, and countless sessions slowly gaining trust in the relationship and course of treatment, SFT goes directly to the presenting issue. While therapists may vary in their approach, the common characteristics which all SFT practitioners embrace are quite simple.

From O'Connell's (2003) *Handbook of Solution-Focused Therapy*, I have combined some of these elements to show their relevance to reference.

- Clients are often capable of solving their own problems.
- Therapists must accept their clients' presentation of their problems.
- The relationship between the clients and therapists is critical to success.
- Goals are focused and attainable in the time available.
- Clients and therapists are on equal basis, but success belongs to the clients.

Clients Are Often Capable of Solving Their Own Problems

It is hard to imagine that anyone who can file a tax form, navigate LA freeways, or raise kids cannot figure out how to find a book on a library shelf. If patrons have difficulty with something so basic, the problem is not with their cognitive ability, but more likely with our materials' arrangement, signage, or directions. Patrons are capable of navigating the library; we just need to assure them that they can. A simple explanation, a map, or a walk with them to the shelves communicates a strong message.

Therapists Must Accept Their Clients' Presentation of Their Problems

"I can get the abstract of the article, but can never get the whole thing. I must be doing something wrong." Librarians have heard this refrain or some variation countless times. It is very likely that the student is doing everything correctly, and it is the library that is causing the student's frustration. The Counselor Librarian must first acknowledge the student's frustration through empathetic listening, and then assure her that she is probably not doing anything wrong. We can review the search process with her, let her guide us through the steps, and let her discover where she may have gone astray, or where the library may have gone astray. By dealing with her immediate problem, we have acknowledged and addressed her concern and established enough trust to locate the breakdown in the search process. The library literature details many instances where the questioner's vagueness or inability to articulate a need is problematic to the process. It should be of no surprise that many other professions, including counseling, face the same issue. As Cormier and Cormier (1991, 178) state, "often clients will initially describe only one problem, and on further inquiry and discussion, the counselor discovers a host of other problems, some of which are more severe or stressful or have greater significance that the one the client originally described."

The Relationship Between the Clients and Therapists is Critical to Success
During the time that Maxfield was implementing the Counselor Librarian model at UIC, Rogers (1957) was writing about the core conditions for establishing a sound therapeutic relationship. He focused on the three essential ingredients needed for a strong, healthy bond between counselor and client: empathy (listen, believe and acknowledge), respect (unconditional positive regard), and genuineness (congruence). Many librarians know what it is like to carry eighteen credit hours, work part-time, and have family responsibilities. Many librarians have the same frustrations with the library system as the students. As customer service providers, librarians tend to be naturally empathetic; however, respect for the student library user can be more difficult to retain. It is difficult to hold a high opinion of the student who comes to the library for research assistance four hours before his paper is due. It is difficult to show unconditional positive regard (a popular counseling phrase) toward a student who wants to find information that conflicts with your personal beliefs. While we should not be ingenuous in our communication (students see through that in a minute), we can be congruent in our interest in helping, despite a lack of enthusiasm for a particular topic.

In SFT there is not much time; in reference there is even less. Still, in both, there can be no therapy if there is no bond. Furthermore, these bonds are not fleeting. While we may interact briefly with a student, how we interact can alter how that student feels about librarians, libraries, and information in the future. Counseling calls this phenomenon transference. Miles, my son-on-law, a Ph.D. student at one of the nation's most prestigious universities, is certain that all librarians are "out to get him." One too many unpleasant, uncooperative, non-empathetic, and unsuccessful library encounters have convinced him that he is better off in the library on his own. In the unlikely event that he seeks a librarian's help, he is going to bring his grievances with him. Helpful librarians need to be sensitive to these past experiences, acknowledge them, and move forward. Of course, the opposite phenomenon (counter-transference) can occur when the librarian's past experiences influence the therapeutic bond. You may find that how you interact with a particular student is influenced by past experiences with similar students. For example, Lucia comes to your office late with a jumble of papers, a bulging backpack, and in general confusion. She reminds you of other students who lack organizational skills and a systematic approach to research. Your tendency may be to begin addressing those issues rather than the ones she is actually presenting. Furthermore, if your experience with similar students has been negative, you may transfer some of those feelings to her, thereby corrupting a healthy relationship before you even start.

A perceptive and empathetic librarian, aware that counter-transference may be taking place, can use this awareness as a clue to better understand the client, and can thereby provide better intervention. In the case of my son-in-law, the Counselor Librarian can identify and address Miles' negative history of unsatisfactory library experiences. In Lucia's case, the librarian may point out that Lucia seems disorganized but should pay close attention to how she responds. If Lucia is aware of her behavior and does not see it as a problem, neither should the librarian.

Goals are Focused and Attainable in the Time Available
As O'Connell (1993, 48) states, "It is the task of the therapist to help the client define her problem in a solvable way and to generate clear, simple, attainable goals for therapy."

Replace counseling words with library words and the statement looks like this, "It is the task of the librarian to help the student define her problem in a solvable way and to generate clear, simple, attainable goals for research." Compare this revised sentence with some of the outcomes in ACRL's *Information Competency Standards for Higher Education*, and you will see an uncanny match.

In SFT the counselor and client must agree on the goals of therapy quickly. Unlike more traditional therapeutic models, which have the luxury of dozens of 50-minute sessions, goal setting in SFT (and reference) must be fast-tracked. In the library, the librarian might say, "It looks like you have lots of research ahead of you and not much time. Tell me what you would like to do first."

Another way to help establish or rank goals is to ask what is often called the "Miracle Question." A counselor might say, "If you woke up tomorrow morning and all of your problems were gone, what specifically would be different?" or, "You are telling me that there are many issues you would like us to address. If you had to rank them on a scale of 1 to 10, which ones would be over 5?" In the library, the Miracle Question is a way to have students imagine what they want. When I am having a particularly difficult time understanding what a student is trying to articulate, I ask, "If you found the perfect journal article for your paper, what would the title be?" or, "Imagine your paper is done and your professor has asked you to tell the class what it is about. What would you say?"

Clients and Therapists are on Equal basis, but Success Belongs to the Clients
In the action therapies of the 1970s and the current postmodern approaches (including SFT), the strength of the counselor-client relationship is the key to

success. The strength of that relationship is the equality between the counselor and the client. Unlike earlier therapeutic approaches where the counselor is the authority, advice giver, and problem solver, SFT views the counselor and counselee as equal partners in a process. This is not to suggest that the counselor (or librarian) is less knowledgeable or experienced than the client or student, but rather that the relationship is built on parity and respect for each other. Both approach the interaction with their own sets of strengths. In counseling, the professional's role is to facilitate a conversation with a specific purpose. In reference it is exactly the same, except that the purpose is much more pragmatic and concrete. Finding journal articles is a lot easier than finding happiness!

According to Cormier and Cormier, use of "action responses" in a therapeutic situation can help move a conversation along without shifting the balance of the relationship. They suggest four such responses which will sound very familiar to librarians: "A *probe* is an open or closed question or inquiry. A *confrontation* is a description of a client discrepancy. An *interpretation* is a possible explanation for the client's behavior. *Information giving* is the communication of data or facts…" (Cormier and Cormier 1991, 121).

The library literature is loaded with talk about open and closed questions or probes. As with all communication tools, probes can be extremely effective. Ask *what* when you want facts from a student ("What class is this for?") This approach will not only save you time, but help to steer the conversation in the most relevant direction. Ask *how* when you are concerned about the process the student has taken to get where she is ("How did you find these articles?") If she tells you that she got them from JSTOR, she has revealed something different than if she said she got them from her professor. Ask *why* when you need to know the student's motivation for the question ("Why are you looking for articles written in 1987?") Perhaps she is doing research on the Iran-Contra Affair and thinks that the only information available is from the time of the scandal. Perhaps she has to find a newspaper headline from the day she was born.

Librarians should probe for information carefully. Otherwise, the interaction can turn into an interrogation, which can sabotage the equilibrium.

Here is a specific example of "action responses." A student is flustered because she cannot find more information on her topic. She tells me that she searched *PsycInfo, Dissertation Abstracts, ERIC, Google Scholar, Music Index*, and several library catalogs. She talked to her professor and has 15 items on her "preliminary bibliography," but she is sure she is missing something. *Probe*: "How long is your paper supposed to be?" I ask. "Five pages," she replies. *Confrontation*: "You're telling me you think you're missing some vital information on your topic, but you seem to have more than enough. *Interpretation*: "Have you thought that you may be avoiding the real purpose of the assignment, which is to write a paper?" *Information Giving*: "If you think it would help, we could review what you have so far and look for any apparent gaps, then, if you have time, we could talk about ways to get you writing." These examples of action responses are direct, but should be used sparingly.

For the sake of illustration take a quick look at an especially bad, though not unlikely, interchange between a librarian and a student, and compare it with the same situation using an SFT approach.

After a couple of minutes wandering around the library, Julie approaches the reference desk.

Traditional Approach

Librarian:	What can I do for you?
Julie:	I need to find some articles.
Librarian:	Okay. Where have you looked so far?
Julie:	I found some online.
Librarian:	Online?
Julie:	Yeah. I found them and sent them to my e-mail but they don't open.
Librarian:	What class is this for?
Julie:	BIO 10. *She rustles through her backpack and pulls out a printed copy of an e-mail that shows she has searched Expanded Academic Index and sent herself articles about Alzheimer's.*
Librarian:	Is this the class where you have to write a paper on a disease?
Julie:	Yeah.
Librarian:	How many pages?
Julie:	*Rustling through her papers again and finally pulling out the syllabus.* It says eight to ten pages, double-spaced.
Librarian:	The database you searched is probably not the best one for this. It is a more general one. How come you picked that one and not one of the biology databases? It's for a biology class, right?
Julie:	I don't know. I used it before for one of my other classes.
Librarian:	What aspect of Alzheimer's are you researching? Genetics? Treatment? Care? It's a big topic.
Julie:	Genetics, I guess.
Librarian:	Let me show you *Science Direct*. It's better than *Expanded Academic Index* for this.

Many things are wrong with this interaction, but for now we should focus on the librarian's motivation and ignore the rest. The librarian, in her laser-like, "take no hostages" fashion, is keen on getting to the "why" regardless of the casualties. She is so intent on the presenting issue (finding articles) that she ignores Julie's "felt need" completely and manipulates the transaction to her own prescriptive solution. While the destination may be justified, the journey is not. For Julie, this is interrogation, not dialogue. In her eagerness to help Julie, the librarian neither reassures her that she is in a safe place, nor compliments her accomplishments thus far. She knows what Julie needs and she is going to give it to her. Period.

What follows is an example of the same interaction, but with the librarian employing some SFT techniques. Remember, in the SFT model, the librarian follows the classic steps of brief therapy: acknowledge an understanding of the reason the person came in, compliment the person's efforts and strengths, come to agreement of what the problem is (using appropriate language), mutually agree on a goal and a task and establish a timeframe to accomplish them, and then follow up.

Solution Focused Approach

Librarian:	Hi. *Smiling and saying, "Hello" initiates a positive relationship, but unlike greeters at The GAP, you have to show your sincerity then back it up with expertise.*
Julie:	Hi. *Julie may acknowledge your greeting with eye contact, or a nod, or a verbal response. Your hope is that she sees this as a cue to ask a question. If she does not you need to be a bit more inviting.*
Librarian:	Is there anything I can do to help you this morning? *The question is intended to show your availability and willingness to assist. It is direct and specific. Notice "this morning" implies that you understand there may be some urgency to her visit, and you are acknowledging that. It also implies that you may have seen her in the library on another occasion. Maintain sincerity or you have lost your chance.*
Julie:	I need to find some articles. *She has taken a big step by accepting your invitation for help and revealing her perceived need. In therapeutic situations this is significant.*
Librarian:	Okay. Let's do that. *This statement shows complete, unconditional regard for her felt need. The relationship is established on an equal footing through the use of using "us" instead of "I." You can nonverbally offer her a chair, smile, gesture, etc., to make her feel welcome and glad that she has accepted the partnership.*
Librarian:	Recent journals are on the third floor, arranged by title. Tell me more about what you would like to find. *This statement is an example of information giving, followed by a declarative probe. It is a standard formula in the dialog. It acknowledges the question and tells the client that she has been heard. By following with a mild command, you open another invitation which is non-threatening to the still fragile relationship.*
Julie:	I found some online. *She rustles through her backpack and pulls out a printed copy of an e-mail that shows she has searched Expanded Academic Index and sent herself articles about Alzheimer's. She is not really responding to you in the way you had hoped, but there may be some transference issues.*

Librarian:	Good work! You've been busy. The library has thousands of journals online. I see you are doing something about Alzheimer's. *This is an example of positive reinforcement plus more information giving. In her own way she has told you what she is looking for. You also have discovered that she has somewhat successfully used a library database and knows how to send articles to her e-mail. You leave room for her to reveal more.*
Julie:	Yeah. *She is not talking much because she still may not feel confident in what she is doing, or sure what you think of her. She is still vulnerable.*
Librarian:	My dad had Alzheimer's. It's horrible on the patient and the family. Pause to give her some time to reply. Would you like to find more articles like the one you found online? *You reveal something about yourself to appear more open to her. By showing something personal, you indicate your humanness and understanding of the issue. Also, you bring up a way the topic could be narrowed (i.e. family issues) to try and get a response from her regarding which aspect of Alzheimer's she may be researching. Some librarians may not be at all comfortable with this. This scenario is an example of information giving followed by probe.*
Julie:	*Rustling through her papers again and finally pulling out the syllabus.* Yeah, it says I need to find at least five sources. This one is good but I need more. When I clicked on them I couldn't get the whole thing. *This is the most she has said so far, and it may be because she is feeling safe with you because you revealed something personal, or she is in a hurry, or she just wants to get started. Watch for non-verbal cues.*
Librarian:	That happens. Sometimes the database has the whole article, sometimes it doesn't. It would be great if they were all online! What class is this for? *With this statement you have provided acknowledgment (with an indication that she is doing nothing wrong) followed by information giving and a probe. She has the syllabus in front of her, so your hope is that she will show it to you. Time is fleeting, and one glance at the assignment will answer many of your questions.*
Julie:	BIO 10. We have to pick something from the list and then write a five page paper about it. He said we can't use the Internet, but it's okay to use magazines. *She is becoming more talkative and seems at ease responding to your probes and revealing information which she may know would help you to help her. This is great progress. It may have been easier for you just to ask for the syllabus, but you may not want to press that just yet.*

Librarian:	There have been several people in from that class this week doing different topics and we found plenty of sources. I'm sure you'll find lots of articles on Alzheimer's, too. My guess is your instructor wants you to use articles because some of the stuff on the Web is not very good. *You are reinforcing that she is not alone; others have had success and so will she. Notice that I use the word "stuff" and "good" rather than introducing new vocabulary and concepts (e.g. sites and credibility). We have set the goals and they are achievable. You have also provided some interpretation of the issue.*
Julie:	Yeah. He said it was okay to use a Web site if he approved it. *She's now revealing more information that expands the problem as she originally presented it.*
Librarian:	Good. Let's take care of the articles first and if we have time I can show you a few Web tricks to get to the reputable sites. Is that okay? *Now you have provided acknowledgement, re-set goals, and set time limits. Remember, this is short term work. You need buy in from her to proceed with the plan you both have established.*
Julie:	Okay. I have about fifteen minutes now, and then I have to get to class. *She has accepted the plan and provided you with the amount of time she can commit.*
Librarian:	Perfect. We shouldn't have any trouble finding what you need. And, if we don't finish it now, you can stop by later, or e-mail me. *You accept her time limits and leave her space to come back or e-mail you for more.*

In the preceding example, the librarian immediately answers the question. The fact that it may not be the right answer because the question is not specific is irrelevant. The message to the student is, "I heard what you asked. I am acknowledging it by giving you an immediate response." Immediacy is critical in SFT and crucial in effective reference work. Helen Gothberg (1976, 128) reported on a study which found that students expressed greater satisfaction with both reference and with *their own performance* (emphasis mine) when librarians communicated with them immediately in both verbal and nonverbal ways.

To one degree or another, many librarians practice SF reference now. What we call it, or how we articulate the model to our own situations, is not as important as the effect it has on those we help. The library literature is brimming with examples of reference librarians' efforts to improve their professional effectiveness. Thirty years ago Rothstein chronicled one hundred years of reference encounters (Katz, et al. 1989). Twenty years ago Jennerich and Jennerich (1987) wrote about the art of reference. Today, we discuss abandoning the physical desk in favor of a virtual one, shifting our reference approach from informative to consultative, and practicing reference by walking around. These and other ideas are certainly well intended, but unless they are built on a totally new belief system, we are simply changing the surface approaches to what we do and ignoring the deeper opportunity. Can a reference avatar provide better help than her corporeal maker? In fact, I worry that the attention we give to new technology and our complete buy-in to a consumer model of library service may have already advanced to the point where they are beyond challenging. After all, Alvin Toffler, who has written extensively on social change, warned us years ago that our social and personal cultures evolve more slowly than our technological ones. He was right, and perhaps the gap is already too wide for us to bridge, but perhaps by realigning our foundations we can find a better connection between reference librarians and those we want to help. Perhaps we have an opportunity to revisit Maxfield's model of the Counselor Librarian and realize that this is where reference belongs.

Sources for Additional Research

Bishop, W. 1999. Questions as interventions: Perceptions of Socratic, solution focused, and diagnostic questioning styles. *Journal of Rational-Emotive & Cognitive-Behavior Therapy* 17 (2): 115-140.
> This article reports on a study of three approaches to questioning, including solution focused. Though a bit technical, the noteworthy conclusion for reference librarians is that most subjects (undergraduate students) ranked solution focused approaches as more straightforward and conducive to independent thinking and problem solving.

Corey, G. 2004. *Theory and practice of counseling and psychotherapy.* 7th ed. Belmont: Brooks/Cole-Thomson Learning.
> Now in the 7th edition, Corey's text is standard reading for students of counseling throughout the U.S. The sections on cognitive based therapies are especially useful for librarians, and his case studies approach is similar to reference situations.

Maxfield, D. K. March 1954. Counselor librarianship: A new departure. In *University of Illinois Library School Occasional Papers.* Chicago: University of Illinois.
> This is the seminal work for the Counselor Librarian model. Though not readily or easily available, this issue of the Occasional Papers from the University of Illinois provides a glimpse into a golden age of librarianship and a new model of reference service.

Penland, P. P. 1971. Counselor Librarianship. In *Encyclopedia of Library and Information Science*, eds. A. Kent and H. Lancour. New York: Marcel Dekker.
> Penland's background and interest in interpersonal communication, adult education and reference come together in this contribution to the first edition of ELIS. He includes a significant historical introduction and explanation of the Counselor Librarian model and a look at the nearly two decades which followed its demise.

Talmon, M. 1990. *Single-session therapy: Maximizing the effect of the first (and often only) therapeutic encounter.* San Francisco: Jossey-Bass.

Talmon condenses his years of experience with single session therapy (an off-shoot of Solution Focused Therapy) into a very practical approach to counseling. Written primarily for those in practice, this small book provides useful illustrations for taking a client through the helping process.

Works Cited

Brammer, L. M., P. J. Abrego, and E. L. Shostrom. 1993. *Therapeutic counseling and psychotherapy.* Upper Saddle River, NJ: Prentice Hall.

Corey, G. 2004. *Theory and practice of counseling and psychotherapy.* 7th ed. Belmont, MA: Brooks/Cole-Thomson.

Cormier, W. H., and S. Cormier. 1991. *Interviewing strategies for helpers: Fundamental skills and cognitive behavioral interventions.* 3rd ed. Pacific Grove, CA: Brooks/Cole.

Gothberg, H. 1976. Immediacy: A study of communication effect on the reference process. *Journal of Academic Librarianship* 2 (3): 126-129.

Hansen, J. C., R. R. Stevic, and R. W. Warner. 1977. *Counseling: Theory and process.* 2nd ed. Boston: Allyn & Bacon.

Harvard University. 1945. *General education in a free society: Report of the Harvard Committee.* Cambridge: Harvard University.

Jennerich, E. Z., and E. J. Jennerich. 1987. *The reference interview as a creative art.* Littleton, CO: Libraries Unlimited.

Katz, W., C. A. Bunge, and S. Rothstein, eds. 1989. *Rothstein on reference: With some help from friends.* New York: Haworth Press.

Lukenbill, W. B. 1983. The Counselor Librarian: Fad or new role for youth librarians? *Top of the News* 40 (1): 81-90.

Maxfield, D. K. 1954a. Counselor Librarianship: A new departure, in *University of Illinois Library School Occasional Papers.* Chicago: University of Illinois.

Maxfield, D. K. 1954b. Counselor Librarianship at UIC. *College and Research Libraries* 15: 161-166, 179.

O'Connell, B., and S. Palmer, eds. 2003. *Handbook of solution-focused therapy.* London: Sage Publications.

Penland, P. P. 1971. Counselor librarianship. In *Encyclopedia of Library and Information Science,* ed. A Kent. New York: Marcel.

Rogers, C.R. 1957. The necessary and sufficient conditions of therapeutic personality change. *Journal of Consulting Psychology* 21: 95-103.

University of Illinois, Chicago. Undergraduate Division. 1948-49. *Library: Annual Report,* No. 3. Chicago: University of Illinois.

Weikel, W.J., A. J. Palmo, and D. P. Borsos, eds. 2006. *Foundations of mental health counseling.* Springfield IL: Charles C. Thomas.

CHAPTER 5

Embedded Library, Embedded Librarian: Strategies for Providing Reference Services in Online Courseware

Meredith G. Farkas

Distance education programs have been offered by academic institutions since long before the birth of the Web, but they did not really become a mainstream educational option until the technologies available to support them matured. While twenty years ago people in geographically isolated areas were the primary users of distance learning, it is now utilized by people all over the country; even those who happen to live close to academic institutions. The convenience of online learning allows people to balance work, family, and education much more easily than many face-to-face programs. With the rapid improvements in social technologies, the negatives associated with online learning—such as lack of community and tacit learning—are decreasing every day.

The growth of online learning in the past few years has been extensive. According to the Sloan Consortium report, *Making the Grade: Online Education in the United States 2006*, in 2002, approximately 1.6 million students were taking at least one online course. By 2005, that had almost doubled to 3.18 million (Allen and Seaman 2006, 5). Some of these students are in completely online programs, where they may never visit a campus during their education. Others take part in hybrid programs that offer a mix of online and face-to-face courses. The opportunities for online education are increasing with the demand. Approximately sixty-three percent of institutions surveyed offered at least some online courses (8). In addition to online courses, many face-to-face classes offer an online component through course management systems.

For online students, the central unit of their learning experience is the course management system they use. This system could be considered the online equivalent of a campus, as it is the space in which students take their classes, submit their papers, and socialize with their peers. While their program may also have a Web site, the real work goes on in the course management system and often, this is the only space online students visit.

Libraries have a long tradition of providing outreach. Whether they are driving a bookmobile, staffing a booth at a consumer health fair, or providing assistance inside the classroom, librarians frequently provide traditional library services outside the walls of the library. In an age when our patrons often access library services online, rather than at a physical location, it becomes all the more important to think about outreach. Many libraries have worked hard to develop a Web presence and to translate traditional library services into the online medium, but some have ignored the importance of providing outreach to online learners.

The Association of College and Research Libraries (ACRL) drafted *Guidelines for Distance Learning Library Services* in 2004 to ensure that equitable library services are provided for all students and faculty. The Guidelines outline the responsibilities of libraries and academic institutions for providing services and allocating funding and personnel to serve the information needs of distance learners. The document is quite comprehensive, but can be summed up in this sentence: "Effective and appropriate services for distance learning communities may differ from, but must be equivalent to, those services offered on a traditional campus" (ACRL 2004). Thus, librarians need to seriously consider how to provide services to online learners and how to make those services just as accessible to them as they are to on-campus students.

This chapter explores the possibilities for embedding library services in online course management systems, including the creation of portals to library services for online learners. While technology is always an issue, many of these strategies are decidedly low-tech, but "high-touch," putting a human face on what was before a faceless edifice. Embedding the library within the course management system streamlines access for online learners, making it more likely that they will utilize library resources and services.

Background on Course Management Systems and Services to Distance Learners

As mentioned before, online learners primarily interact with colleges or universities through a course management system. A course management system (CMS) may also be referred to as a learning management system, a virtual learning environment, or online courseware. It is essentially a piece of software or a suite of software tools that enables every aspect of course management and delivery. They include the ability to post readings, announcements, assignments, quizzes and learning objects, take part in synchronous and asynchronous discussions, use automated grading tools, and much more. These systems can be more or less full-featured, and there are open source options in addition to those offered by large corporate entities.

While there were virtual learning environments in existence before the graphical Web, the CMS as we know it was first introduced in the mid-1990s. Initially, many colleges and universities were engaged in developing their own CMSs, but by 2000, much of the development was occurring in the corporate sector. These systems were usually commercialized versions of the most successful university CMSs, such as *WebCT* (built at the University of British Columbia) and *Blackboard* (built at Cornell University). While some academic institutions still use their own homegrown systems and there are dozens of commercial systems, the market is dominated by six major players: *Blackboard* and *WebCT* (which merged in 2005), *Angel, Moodle, Desire2Learn* and *Sakai* (Gibbons 2005, 7-10).

While these systems were being developed, most libraries were not waiting for opportunities to provide reference and instruction services to online learners. Although some libraries did not alter their services as their school's distance learning opportunities grew, there are examples in the literature of libraries that were on the cutting edge in providing support services to distance learners in the 1980s and 1990s. 1 The Distance Learning Section of ACRL was formed in 1990, a recognition of the importance of providing services to this growing population. By the mid-1990s, most libraries offered reference services via e-mail, and later in the decade, some were also providing synchronous online reference assistance through commercial tools and instant messaging. Other libraries were providing instruction using video teleconferencing, which was in its infancy at the time. Information literacy instruction and course materials were also provided via CD-ROM and the Web. As the number of databases available online increased, librarians had to learn how to provide assistance and instruction in using these new tools.

At the same time, librarians were also exploring how to personalize online library services for different populations. The late 1990s saw the growing popularity of portals, which in the library world manifested as the MyLibrary movement. MyLibrary was a system developed at North Carolina State University that allowed libraries to create customized user-interfaces for different populations. These interfaces usually included listings of books, journals, databases, and Web sites that were useful to that population. Many other libraries developed similar database-driven systems which made it far easier for librarians to create subject pathfinders and course guides. A few of these systems even allowed users to create their own personalized pages of resources. Libraries without the technology support developed similar subject pages using HTML, but they were not as easy to create or update (Gibbons 2005, 33-37).

While CMS developers and librarians were both engaged in building new technology-driven strategies for providing services to online learners, the groups rarely collaborated. In the 2002 article, "Course Management Software: Where's the Library?" David Cohen presented the results of a study which indicated that CMS vendors did not consider libraries or their resources in development because "libraries were generally not involved in the software-purchase decisions made by their institutions" (Cohen 2002, 13). The fact that the integration of library resources and services was not a priority made it technically difficult for library resources to be integrated into the CMS. This separation created two separate silos of information for students—the library Web site and the CMS. If the CMS is the virtual equivalent of a campus, then the library should have a presence. If a student is required to leave the CMS to find the library, then this is the online equivalent of requiring a student to drive across town to get from the classroom to the library. Students are far more likely to utilize library resources if access to them is seamless.

Creating Portals to Library Services within the Course Management System

Colleges and universities spend significant amounts of money on library collections. Librarians spend significant amounts of time developing online library services, such as synchronous virtual reference and subject guides. If students do not know that these resources and services are available to them, or if they cannot easily access them, then no one is getting much value for their investment. It is crucial for libraries to make their resources and collections as visible as possible, and to make access seamless for all service populations. In the case of online learners, this likely requires creating a library presence in the CMS. While it can take significant effort to achieve library integration with the CMS, the benefits to both the online learner and the library are undeniable.

In their seminal work on this subject, Shank and Dewald (2003) outlined two different models to embed libraries in the CMS. The first, Macro-Level Library Courseware Involvement (MaLLCI), requires the creation of a single global library presence for all online courses. In this model, every online learner sees the exact same library presence (39-40). Macro-level involvement could be as simple as providing a link to the library Web site or to specific resources, such as the online databases, the catalog, a virtual reference page, and research guides. Many libraries have special pages on their Web site designed just for distance learners that provide information unique to their circumstances. While the information provided is valuable, it does not make as much sense to provide this information outside of the CMS. Some libraries have developed unique library Web sites for distance learners that live in the CMS. Sometimes this presence is placed in a content repository where it can be linked to every class. At other times, libraries are given their own online classroom to develop, and the students are all enrolled in this library class. While the latter option certainly gives the librarians more ability to develop learning modules, assessments, and mechanisms for communication, the former option does not require the student to leave his or her primary classroom.

The second model is Micro-Level Library Courseware Involvement (MiLL-CI), which involves a customized library presence at the program or course level. This approach means that each program or course has a list of library resources in its subject area, subject-related tutorials or some other method of instruction, as well as all of the elements that go into a global library presence. Some libraries already have subject guides and micro-level tutorials on their Web sites, so linking to these or moving the content into the CMS is all that is needed (40-41).

There are pros and cons to both models. Obviously, the macro approach requires far less effort and maintenance because there is a single library presence. Librarians do not need to work closely with faculty members in each discipline. As the number of programs and courses offered online grows, a universal presence ensures that the library can continue to provide the same level of service to all programs. On the other hand, the services and resources are not targeted to specific disciplines. A student may look at a long list of databases and have no idea which ones are the best to use for their specific research. Considering how differently research is conducted in each discipline, having a global presence with generic tutorials may not adequately meet the needs of anyone. A lack of subject or course-specific tutorials and resources may lead to more work for the library in the form of individual reference questions from students.

The micro-level approach better meets the needs of students by offering re-sources and services tied to what they are studying. Librarians can provide research help and instruction that mirrors what is offered to on-campus classes. However, this approach requires significantly more time and effort to develop and update resources for every discipline or every class. The micro-level approach also requires librarians to collaborate more closely with faculty, since faculty members are the true content experts. This collaboration can be an excellent opportunity to make the library a more visible player in that discipline and to integrate information literacy instruction into the curriculum. On the other hand, if a faculty member is not interested in collaborating, the librarian may have a difficult time achieving the micro-level approach. Some faculty members may not see the value of library services in their courses. They may even see the librarian as trying to take over their instructional role. Librarians need to make a strong case for the involve-ment of the library and make clear what role they play and how that differs from the instructor's role. Sometimes librarians can build relationships at the program level, where department heads and program administrators ensure that the library gets the access and cooperation they need. In other cases, librarians need to build relationships with every individual faculty member that they work with. While this can be time-consuming, a good relationship with faculty ensures not only that the library has access, but that the faculty member understands when to recommend that students seek help from the library.

In his article "Vision and Strategy Towards the Course-Embedded Library" (Sabharwal 2005), Sabharwal articulates a third option: the nano approach. This approach "would target the information architecture" of each individual course. This means that library services are tailored to individual courses based on a thorough assessment of the instructional design of each course. It requires a great deal of collaborative work with both the instructor and the instructional designer working on the course. While this is a noble goal that ensures library resources and services are available at the point of need, it can be too time-consuming for most librarians to take on in every course. This approach does, however, highlight the importance of understanding the design of a course, or group of courses, in order to seamlessly integrate the library presence.

Some libraries adopt a hybrid approach when it comes to building a library presence into the CMS. At Norwich University in Vermont, every classroom links to the same library portal in a WebCT content repository. However, within the portal, there are subject specific database lists, Web links, and tutorials; all acces-sible from drop-down menus. Much of the information that students need—such as the database access FAQ, instructions for making an interlibrary loan request, or information on how to contact a librarian—is common to all disciplines. While that information could be placed into separate library portals for each subject or course, it would require more effort to maintain. With the hybrid approach, if the protocol for requesting materials via interlibrary loan changes, the information only has to be changed in one place, instead of in every class or discipline. When determining which approach to adopt, it is important to consider not only how much effort it will take to create the materials, but what the future maintenance burden might be.

Any of the above approaches require a good relationship with the technology staff who administer the CMS and develop the courses. The instructional technologists control access and will likely only grant administrative access to individuals they trust. At some institutions, the librarians must send content to the technology staff instead of uploading it themselves, which can create a bottleneck in updating content. In settings where there are no librarians with Web design skills, it is possible that the instructional developers can take over the role of developing the library presence, which necessitates an even closer working relationship. Librarians need to build a solid relationship with the technologists so that they can understand the needs of the library and the capabilities of the librarians.

Embedded Librarian Concept

Librarians who have worked for years with students in specific courses or programs are often aware of common problems that crop up as students complete assignments and do research. Usually, however, the librarian must wait for the student to contact the reference desk to be able to provide assistance, and many students do not feel comfortable asking questions of the librarian. Having a librarian embedded in the classroom allows them to provide course specific reference assistance and instruction at the point of need, or even before the need, and really ties the reference services to the curriculum.

There are a variety of ways that this embedded model can take shape. Markgraf (2004) described a "lurking librarian" model, where the librarian scans the discussion threads in the online classroom and provides assistance on the discussion board when an information need presents itself. This model does not require the student to actually ask a question of the librarian, but it does require the librarian to do a great deal of work in identifying points where intervention would be beneficial.

Matthew and Schroeder (2006) describe several ways that a librarian can provide assistance within the classroom. One common way is to create an "Ask a Librarian" discussion board. This virtual space gives the students a single space in which they can ask research-related questions (63). In addition, the librarian can use the discussion board to provide instruction by addressing some of the issues students may encounter in their research. In a history course where students are about to choose their research topics, the librarian may discuss the value of pre-research to determine if there is an appropriate amount of information available on their topics. This intervention may lead to questions from students about the appropriateness of their topics. Librarians can provide instruction on the best resources to use for assignments, how to search specific databases, and much more. They can also avoid answering the same common questions from students over and over again, because everyone in the classroom will be able to view the answers. This practice is valuable for those students who may have the same questions, but do not feel comfortable asking the librarian.

In some classes, the instructor creates weekly *Ask a Librarian* discussion threads where students can ask questions. On the one hand, this indicates to students that the instructor places value on the involvement of the librarian, which might make students more likely to ask questions. On the other hand, in a class where there is not a great deal of research every week, students may not have questions to ask. Matthew and Schroeder describe how some instructors have required students to ask a question of the librarian each week, which led to frivolous questions unrelated to the course material. They also, however, describe courses where the instructor creates *Ask a Librarian* threads only during the weeks where students are required to do research, or only for specific assignments (63-64). The approach chosen for embedding reference services into the classroom really depends on how research intensive the course is and what the instructor expects from the librarian. It is important for faculty members to highlight the value that the librarian brings to the class, because students take their cues from their instructor. If the instructor suggests that students run their paper topics by the librarian before they are approved, the students will be more likely to do so than in a class where the professor never mentions the librarian.

Probably the biggest problem with any of the embedded librarian models is the amount of time required to provide the service. Librarians embedded in online classrooms may need to check each one at least once a day and answer questions. Markgraf's lurker model and classes where the students are required to ask weekly questions of the librarian are likely going to be the most time-consuming. If time is a factor, it may make sense to only have *Ask a Librarian* discussion threads in specific weeks where students would likely need the librarian, such as when they are choosing a topic, doing their initial research, creating a bibliography, and writing the paper.

Future of Libraries and Librarians in the Course Management System

Looking at most of the popular CMSs, it is apparent that library resources and services were not considered in their design. While there are modules for the easy integration of many aspects of a typical academic course, ingenuity is required on the part of the librarian and instructional designer to actually integrate library resources and services into the CMS. At many universities, where librarians either do not have the requisite tech-savvy or access, there is no library integration, and online learners must simply visit the library Web site to get what they need. In an increasingly saturated distance education market, one thing that can set a program apart is its library's resources and services. However, if these are not well-integrated into the CMS, it is almost the same as not having the resources at all. In the future, it is likely that most colleges and universities will demand (or build their own) extensions to the traditional CMS, which will better integrate library resources and services.

One current barrier to librarian involvement in course management systems is the lack of granular permissions. For librarians to be able to add and edit library content in the CMS, they often need to have full administrative access to the course. While some systems offer user roles with limited access, in many cases, access is an all or nothing proposition. If the instructional designers or faculty members do not feel comfortable with a librarian having that level of access, they will lose the opportunity to provide quality library services within the CMS. With some systems, librarians need to be registered for the class as an instructor to staff their own discussion board. This level of access is something not every faculty member will be comfortable with, and it may also be confusing for the students who will be unsure to whom they should direct their questions. Newer iterations of popular course management systems have more user roles available, but only a few have made it easy for librarians to provide services in the CMS.

Course management systems are likely to be more fully integrated with library resources in the future. Until now, universities have had to develop their own tools to better link library resources into the classroom. *RefWorks* and Northwestern University worked to create a *Blackboard* extension that links *RefWorks* to *Blackboard* (Gibbons 2005, 25-26). Penn State University has developed tools that automatically link electronic reserve readings and subject or course guides in the classroom, making access far more seamless for students. These tools have made it easier for librarians to get this material into the CMS without high-level technology skills (Snavely and Smith 2003, 1-3). Just as commercial CMSs grew out of homegrown systems, course management systems will probably adopt these CMS "extensions" for wider use. For CMS vendors to stay competitive, they will have to make it easier for librarians to develop portals to library resources and services and for instructors to use library resources in the classroom.

Libraries will also continue to adapt to changes in the online learning landscape. Many libraries are only starting to provide services to online learners that are distinct from those provided to their on-campus students. Providing services to online learners requires a re-imagining of library services. For example, libraries that have traditionally provided reference services during "business hours" will find that most online learners are doing their research on nights and weekends. Many libraries have responded to the growth of distance learning by hiring librarians specifically to work with that population. In 2004, a survey of Association of Research Libraries institutions that provide services to distance learners found that twenty-one percent had a full-time distance learning librarian and thirty-five percent had someone for whom distance learning support is a part of their job duties (Yang 2005, 93-4). At schools where distance learners make up a significant portion of the population, a full-time distance learning librarian is needed to provide equitable services to these students.

In addition to hiring distance learning librarians, libraries have made the hiring of librarians with higher-level technology skills a priority. These days, librarians are graduating from library school with skills in Web design, database administration, and network administration. When librarians have both library and technology skills, they are better able to develop online services for distance learners. Some librarians or library support staff can even develop applications to extend the functionality of library resources or the CMS. These librarians can often act as liaisons to the instructional designers and information technology staff, because they often have similar skill-sets and "speak the same language." If instructional designers know that librarians are proficient in Web design, they will likely feel more comfortable giving them access to the CMS.

Over the past few years, social software has become a mainstream part of many individuals' online lives. By 2006, people were posting 1.6 million blog posts per day and more than fifty million blogs had been created (Sifry 2006). Wikis, instant messaging, and social networking software are not only used by young people to communicate and collaborate, but also by businesses and non-profit institutions. It has become far more common to see social software in use in educational contexts as well. Faculty are using blogs, wikis, RSS, and podcasting in order to provide a richer learning experience. Online learners who are geographically distant from one another are building communities outside of the CMS using tools such as *Facebook* (www.facebook.com), *Google Groups* (groups.google.com), and *LiveJournal* (www.livejournal.com). People are finding that the CMS does not always provide the functionality that they need to create the collaborative environment and sense of community that many want from an online course.

The creators of popular course management systems have started looking at how they can integrate social software tools into the CMS. *Elgg* (elgg.org) is an open source social networking tool that includes profiles, blogs, wikis, RSS and more. In 2006, they worked with one of the founders of *WebCT* to integrate their product with the CMS. *Blackboard* opened up its API (Application Programming Interface) to some developers of complementary products so that they could better integrate their products with *Blackboard*. As a result, Learning Objects (www.learningobjects.com) developed a *Blackboard Building Block*—a for-pay add-on to the basic *Blackboard* package—which provides blogs, wikis and podcasting support within *Blackboard*. In 2007, *Angel* announced that ANGEL LMS 7.2 would also provide blogs, wikis and podcasting support, but as part of their basic software package.

Conclusion

As libraries begin to adapt to providing services for distance learners, and CMS developers adapt to the demand for better integration with library resources and social software tools, embedding library services into *WebCT* and other systems will become easier. When social tools begin to be more closely integrated into the CMS, libraries will no longer need to depend on outside tools to communicate with and push information to their online patrons. As librarians develop stronger technology skills, they will be better equipped to work closely with instructional designers to ensure that the library is an integral part of every online classroom. They may also be able to design their own creative solutions when their CMS does not provide the functionality they need. Technologies notwithstanding, librarians will still need to build rapport with faculty members and instructional designers to ensure that library presence is considered when courses are developed. Librarians need to be talented marketers of library resources and services in order to ensure that they are able to provide the best possible services to online learners.

Sources for Additional Research

Cohen, D. 2002. Course management software: Where's the library? *Educause Review* 37 (3): 12-13.

> Cohen shares findings from an Academic Library Advisory Committee survey which found that CMS vendors generally overlooked the library during software development. He suggests that this disconnect between the library and the online courseware can lead to decreased student usage of library resources.

Gibbons, S. 2005. Library course-management systems: An overview. *Library Technology Reports* 41 (3).

> In this fifty-two page technology report, Gibbons presents a comprehensive look at course management systems and the issues involved in building a library presence for online learners—whether in the CMS or outside. The author surveys the possibilities and barriers involved in embedding library resources into the course management system, both technical and cultural, and offers many concrete examples of libraries that have successfully integrated the library into the CMS.

Markgraf, J. 2004. Librarian participation in the online classroom. *Internet Reference Services Quarterly* 9 (1/2): 5-19.

> Markgraf chronicles her experiences as a "lurking librarian" in the distance learning classroom, and discusses providing reference services at the point of need on class discussion boards. The importance of faculty-librarian cooperation is highlighted in this article, as are the author's insights into the needs and expectations of distance learners.

Matthew, V. and A. Schroeder. 2006. The embedded librarian program. *Educause Quarterly* 29 (4): 61- 65.

> Matthew, the instructor, and Schroeder, the librarian, describe how they shaped the successful embedded librarian program at the Community College of Vermont. The authors describe the various models for librarian involvement in the classroom, suggest ways that this collaboration can be most successful, and suggest things to avoid. The article also discusses the use of videoconferencing in providing information literacy instruction.

Sabharwal, A. 2005. Vision and strategy towards the course-embedded library: New possibilities for a "virtual carrel" initiative. *MLA Forum* 4 (1). http://www.mlaforum. org/volumeIV/issue2/article3.html.

> This article provides an excellent review of the literature on the subject of embedding library services into online courseware. Sabharwal discusses Shank and Dewald's (2003) macro- and micro-level models of library presence, and suggests his own nano-level strategy for seamless library integration in the CMS. In his approach, library presence is designed on the course level, but requires a keen understanding of the information architecture of the classroom so that the library design is consistent with the course design.

Shank, John and S. Bell. 2006. A_FLIP to courseware: A strategic alliance for improving student learning outcomes. *Innovate: Journal of Online Education* 2 (4). http://www.innovateonline.info/index.php?view=article&id=46.

The authors discuss the difficulties involved in developing a library presence within the CMS. They also suggest a model for building cooperation among librarians and courseware administrators called A_FLIP (Administrators, Faculty, Librarians Instructional Partnership). Finally, they describe the importance of working collaboratively with instructional designers and faculty members to create either a global library presence in the CMS or a presence designed for specific courses.

Shank, J. D. and N. H. Dewald. 2003. Establishing our presence in courseware: Adding library services to the virtual classroom. *Information Technology and Libraries* 22 (1): 38-43.

In this seminal work on the topic, Shank and Dewald suggest two models for building a library presence in online courseware in order to increase the visibility of library resources and services. They describe the macro- and micro-level approaches, which prescribe a global presence and a course-based presence respectively, and discuss the pros and cons of each approach.

York, A. 2006. The embedded librarian service at MTSU. *Tennessee Libraries* 56 (2). http://www.tnla.org/displaycommon.cfm?an=1&subarticlenbr=65.

Published as part of a presentation entitled "Distance education and its impact on the academic library," this article offers a practical view into one library's attempt to embed library services into the online courseware. York discusses the problems libraries face in trying to provide quality services to online learners, and presents the embedded librarian service as a solution.

Works Cited

Allen, E. and J. Seaman. 2006. *Making the Grade: Online Education in the United States, 2006.* Needham, MA: Sloan-C. http://www.sloan-c.org/publications/survey/pdf/making_the_grade.pdf.

Association of College & Research Libraries (ACRL). 2004. Guidelines for distance learning library services. http://www.ala.org/ala/acrl/acrlstandards/guidelinesdistancelearning.htm.

Cohen, D. 2002. Course management software: Where's the library? *Educause Review* 37 (3): 12-13.

Gibbons, S. 2005. Library course-management systems: An overview. *Library Technology Reports* 41 (3): 46-49.

Markgraf, J. 2004. Librarian participation in the online classroom. *Internet Reference Services Quarterly* 9 (1/2): 5-19.

Matthew, V. and A. Schroeder. 2006. The embedded librarian program. *Educause Quarterly* 29 (4): 61-65.

Shank, J. D. and N. H. Dewald. 2003. Establishing our presence in courseware: Adding library services to the virtual classroom. *Information Technology and Libraries* 22 (1): 38-43.

Sifry, David. 2006. State of the blogosphere, August 2006. *Sifry's Alerts.* http://www.sifry.com/alerts/archives/000436.html.

Snavely, L. and H. Smith. 2003. Bringing the library to students: Linking customized library resources through a course-management system. Paper Presented at the ACRL Eleventh National Conference, Charlotte, North Carolina, April 10-13, 2003. http://www.ala.org/ala/acrl/acrlevents/snavelysmith.PDF.

Yang, Z. Y. 2005. Distance education librarians in the U.S. ARL libraries and library services provided to distance learners. *The Journal of Academic Librarianship* 31 (2): 92-7.

Notes

1. An excellent bibliography that covers many of the papers presented in the 1980s and 1990s at the Off-Campus Library Services conference is at Reiten, B. A. and J. Fritts. 2006. "Distance Learning Library Services Potential Literature bibliography." Paper presented at The Twelfth Off-Campus Library Services Conference, Savannah, Georgia, April 26-28, 2006. http://e-archive.library.okstate.edu/ocls/3/ (accessed November 6, 2007). Reiten and Fritts also compiled a bibliography of historical core literature on distance learning library services from the 1970s and 1980s, which can be found at the following URL http://e-archive.library.okstate.edu/ocls/5/ (accessed November 7, 2007).

CHAPTER 6

The IM Cometh: The Future of Chat Reference

Stephen Francoeur

It has been over a decade since librarians first began offering chat reference services to their users. Over the years, librarians have explored a variety of options for providing live online reference. There are chat services that are designed to help users from just one library and others that are intended to help users from a group of libraries. Some libraries restrict questions to ready reference, while others take all questions. There are librarians who monitor the service from reference desks, librarians who only do chat from staff offices, and even some that monitor accounts from a centralized reference center. Librarians have also employed many different technologies which allow them to exchange text-based messages with library users in real time: MOOs, MUDs, IRC, chat rooms, instant messaging, commercial Web-based chat software, VoIP software, and video software with chat components (Francoeur 2001; Sloan 2006). In short, the last ten years have been an era of experimentation and innovation for chat reference services. Currently, the majority of academic libraries that provide chat reference have set up their services along one of these three models:

- the library has its own subscription to Web-based chat software (such as OCLC's *QuestionPoint,* Docutek's *VRL,* or *LivePerson*), does not participate in a chat reference cooperative, and offers limited hours of service
- the library has set up its own screen names in one or more commercial instant messaging services (such as AOL *IM,* Yahoo! *Messenger*, MSN *Messenger*), monitors only those screen names, and offers limited hours of service
- the library shares a subscription to a Web-based chat software, participates in a chat reference cooperative, and offers lengthy or round-the-clock hours of service

In the late 1990s, there were a considerable number of Internet technologies used to offer chat reference; by the early 2000s, that number had shrunk notably. From recent developments, it appears that the coming years are likely to mark another era of expanding technology choices for how chat reference services can be provided. Those who try to predict such developments accurately, though, do so at their peril, as the pace of technological change has quickened considerably and we begin to enter an environment of ubiquitous computing so well described by Morville in *Ambient Findability* (2005). The ways in which we can offer a chat service are constrained by the technology available. As the technology changes, so too will our services. This chapter analyzes current technology trends and maps how those changes will shape chat reference services in the near future.

Before delving into the trends themselves, it is worth taking a moment to sketch the history of chat services. Sloan's research into the history of virtual reference services suggests that the first library-based chat reference service was launched in 1996 by Michigan State University (2006). From 1996 to 1999, most libraries offering chat reference were using either instant messaging software, chat rooms, or homegrown software (such as that used by Temple University). These years mark the first era of chat reference services, when none of the library vendors were providing chat reference software and the functionality of the available software was limited. A new era of chat reference began in 1999-2000, when libraries first began using robust chat software originally designed for online retailers (such as Lands End and L.L. Bean) who wanted to be able to chat with customers on their Web sites and direct them to specific pages on their sites. These feature-rich chat products generated a great deal of attention in the library world for the next five or six years, as they provided a raft of features that made chat reference seem more respectable and professional. Many libraries signed up for expensive subscriptions to a class of chat technology that will here be referred to as "Web-based chat software."

Glossary

Web-based chat, Chat:
Throughout this chapter, live chat programs like QuestionPoint, LSSI, and Docutek will be referred to as "Web-based chat" or "chat." These feature-rich products frequently offer co-browsing, page pushing, and the ability to form multi-library staffing groups.

Instant Messaging, IM:
Throughout this chapter, live chat programs like AIM, Yahoo!, MSN, and Google Talk will be referred to as "Instant Messengers" or "IM." These light-weight, externally hosted services have been more recently adopted by libraries as a result of their low learning curve and prevalence amongst college-age individuals.

By 2004, though, critics of Web-based chat software found company in growing numbers of librarians who began to view the software as cumbersome, hard to learn, buggy, and expensive. A pair of articles by Coffman and Arret (2004a, 2004b), two early advocates of chat reference and Web-based chat software, questioned whether such services were supportable and instead advocated that libraries expand their telephone reference services to reach offsite users. These articles marked the start of a series of publications that highlighted the failings of expensive software and argued that there was a cheaper, easier way to do chat reference (Tenopir 2004; Forster 2005; Horowitz, Flanagan, and Helman 2005; Houghton and Schmidt 2005; Stephens 2006). With the 2004 release of Windows Service Pack 2 and the concurrent rise of pop-up blockers, firewalls, and alternative browsers not fully supported by Web-based chat software (such as Firefox), many libraries began to report problems with their Web-based chat reference software: users who could not connect, users who were disconnected, and co-browsing that failed (Lupien 2006; McCulley and Reinauer 2006; Pulliam and McCullen 2006; Radford and Kern 2006).

At this point, the number of libraries using instant messaging (IM) software such as AOL's IM began to grow quickly. Some libraries dropped their Web-based chat for IM software. Others just starting out in chat reference only considered IM, while others decided to run IM services parallel to their Web-based one. The era in which Web-based chat software dominated the discussion of chat reference services had come to a close. Based on the increasing number of libraries now using IM for their chat services, it is fair to say that IM software is now seen as an equally valid technology option for providing a chat service (to see the growth of IM software for chat services, take a look at the history of updates to the "Chat reference libraries" page on the *LISWiki*). The future of chat reference begins here, where IM software is now an established and expanding part of the chat reference environment.

Converging Communication Channels
The number of ways to communicate via the Internet has expanded considerably in recent years. The current options include:

- e-mail
- bulletin boards and message boards
- Q&A services (Ask *MetaFilter*, Yahoo! *Answers*, etc.)
- instant messaging
- chat rooms
- social network sites (*Facebook, MySpace*, etc.)
- blogs
- wikis
- Voice over Internet Protocol (*Skype*, etc.)
- Web conferencing/video conferencing

Not only are there many online communication channels, there are many Web services that allow you take messages composed in one channel and transport them over to another. The *New York Times* technology columnist David Pogue reported on forthcoming "systems that [will] unify your communication (voice, text messages, and chat, for example) by giving you a single address book mailbox for all of them" (Pogue 2007). Content composed in one channel can be passed along or republished in many others in a daisy chain: cell phones can be used to send an instant message, which in turn can be converted into text message, which in turn can be converted into a blog post on the Web, which can then be automatically e-mailed out to subscribers or posted to someone's profile page in a social networking site like *Facebook. Twitter* is one such service that takes messages written in one medium and then distributes them broadly across many others. A *Twitter* user can compose a message on her cell phone that is then posted to her *Twitter* page and sent as a text message to any of her friends who have elected to get her updates this way. Her stream of messages also generates an RSS feed that republishes what she has written; that feed can in turn be republished on a blog or on her *Facebook* page.

The convergence and intertwining of communication channels, which is becoming more and more the norm on the Web, offers new opportunities for library reference services. A reference interaction that begins in one channel might be completed in another. Presently, it is not uncommon for a librarian engaged in a chat session to recommend that the patron call the librarian on the phone for more in-depth assistance, or that the patron look for an e-mail from the librarian that offers further advice about the question at hand. As newer communication channels mature, librarians may find a chat session turning into a Voice over Internet Protocol (VoIP) session or a video conference. Many IM clients already include VoIP and video capabilities.

Convergence among instant messaging systems is another notable trend. Initially, the major instant messaging services (AOL *IM,* Yahoo! *Messenger,* and MSN *Messenger*) did not allow users from one service to send messages to another. If you had an AOL IM (*AIM*) account, for example, you were only able to send messages to other *AIM* users. Over the years, the major services have opened up a bit. For example, Yahoo! *Messenger* and MSN *Messenger* (now known as *Windows Live Messenger*) allow messages to and from each other's services. Complete interoperability between all the major services is still in the future, though. A number of companies have recognized the need for a service that would allow people to at least bundle together all their IM accounts in one screen, allowing them to monitor several accounts in one place. A librarian who wants to maximize the number of potential users of the library's IM will likely create accounts and screen names in each of the major services. Using an IM bundling service like *Meebo, Trillian,* or *Pidgin,* allows them to monitor all their accounts at once.

Another notable trend in IM is the rise of the "chat with me now" widget on library Web sites that allows one-to-one chats for users regardless of whether they have IM accounts. Setting up these widgets is simply a matter of creating an account with one of the free Web services (such as those from *Meebo, Plugoo,* or *Chatango*) and copying code provided by the service into pages on your library site. The *MeeboMe* widget from *Meebo* allows the librarian to monitor both the library's IM screen names and its *MeeboMe* widget all from the same interface. As can be seen on the "Online Reference" page in the *Library Success* wiki, there is a long list of libraries using IM bundling services and chat widgets for their chat reference services (2007).

Another aspect of the convergence trend can be seen in the case of the social networking site, *Facebook.* In August 2006, *Facebook* released its application programming interface (API) to the public, allowing developers outside the company to create various widgets that *Facebook* users could add to their profile pages. Some librarians have begun to experiment with these widgets. In 2007, the University of Illinois at Urbana-Champaign created a library widget that anyone can add to their profile page and use to search the catalog or connect with the library's chat reference service. *Meebo* has created a *MeeboMe* widget that can be put on a profile page; this widget might be useful to the academic librarian who wants to create a *Facebook* page and give students a way to chat directly with the librarian. There are also widgets for *Twitter* and a similar service, *Jaiku*, that can be added to *Facebook* pages.

Some chat reference services have set up profile pages in *MySpace*: the statewide services for Maryland (*AskUsNow.org*) and for New Jersey (*QandANJ.org*) and the service for the libraries of the University of Central Florida. It is not certain what percentage of students actually expect to find a profile page for their library, let alone their library's chat service, in *MySpace* (or even add that profile page as a "friend"). Still, the payoff in free advertising for the chat service may alone be worth the minimal effort that it takes a library's staff to set up such a profile in *MySpace*. A survey by Lenhart and Madden (2006) found that fifty-five percent of all youth between the ages of twelve and seventeen use social networking sites. boyd (in press) notes, though, that the real numbers may be higher. She points out that surveys of teens conducted by the Pew Internet and American Life project are done with the child's parent present, a situation in which some teens might be unwilling to admit to to their online activities. Regardless, the number of teens with profiles on online social networking sites is large enough that librarians need to be aware of this cohort of future college students.

Rapid Shifts in Technologies and Services

As librarians try to work with new communication channels on the Web, they must be mindful that what is wildly popular now on the Internet may soon be passé. With the rise of *MySpace* and *Facebook*'s popularity, many librarians have been exploring ways that they can embed themselves in social network sites. Working in these environments presents unique challenges for librarians, as the recent past is littered with social sites whose online traffic grew quickly and then in the course of a year or two cooled off notably (as was the case for *Classmates. com*, *Friendster*, and *Orkut*). Although at the moment, *Facebook*'s trajectory continues to be upward, it is entirely possible it too will be abandoned in the not-too-distant future when much of its audience's attention is captured by some new network. Librarians who want to harness the power of these sites must be prepared for change and instability. Even if a library has invested time in setting up reference services in *Facebook*, for example, the tools it develops there and the lessons it learns about how to do reference in a social network site will likely be useful in whatever is the next big thing online.

One way a librarian can offer reference in *Facebook* is to add a *MeeboMe* widget to the library's institution page or to the pages of individual librarians who have set up profiles. This use of chat widgets on librarian profile pages mirrors a development that is becoming more common on the Web sites of academic libraries: each subject specialist in the library is given his or her own Web page that features not only office phone numbers and e-mail addresses but also chat options; some have links that users can click to initiate direct IM sessions with that librarian, while others feature chat widgets (such as the *MeeboMe* or *Chatango* widgets) that allow anyone to see if that particular librarian is online and available for chat.

Many academic librarians have long given their contact information to students and faculty so that research consultations, impromptu or scheduled, might be set up. The use of chat technology in *Facebook* profile pages or librarian profile pages on library Web sites seems to herald a new way of providing chat reference that would be a bit different from traditional chat services. Imagine a college library Web site, for example, where every librarian has his or her own profile page with a *MeeboMe* widget. Because the pages contain links to individuals' chat widgets in addition to a general chat service, students can speak directly to the most appropriate subject specialist. Additionally, every librarian could have a profile page in *Facebook* that features a *MeeboMe* widget.

A word of caution is advisable: students may not see *Facebook* as being valuable to their research efforts, but instead think of it as a place for socializing. An informal poll conducted by librarians at the University of Michigan on the school's *Facebook* network suggests that social sites are unlikely sites for reference services (Chapman 2007). Students were asked to indicate their "preferred method for getting research help from a librarian" from a list of five choices Out of the two hundred students who responded, the greatest number (59%, n=118) said that they would rather go in person to see a librarian while the smallest number, just one, selected *"Facebook/MySpace/*other social network" as the preferred method of contact. Nineteen percent (n=38) of the students selected "I'm not interested in contacting a librarian;" one has to wonder if some of these respondents felt annoyed that librarians were contemplating being in *Facebook* and so selected this option out of anger or sarcasm. Of the five choices, instant messaging came in fourth place (16%, n=16). Despite the possibility that students are not yet ready to share social networks with anyone but their peers, librarians should be prepared to investigate new social networks as they arise, see what the terms of service are (can a profile page be set up for the library or just librarians), and find ways to use those networks to connect students to the chat services of both the library and of specific librarians who are subject specialists.

The bewildering array of new Web services and tools in recent years tends to overshadow the instabilities in the process of Web evolution. One phenomenon that is not widely reported is the much-heralded launch of a Web site that later fails. Librarians who are trying to build their new services based on emerging Web services should keep in mind that some sites do not endure. Consider, for example, the closure of a Web service that seemed to hold great promise for chat reference services: *Jybe*. In 2005, a number of librarians were touting *Jybe* as a great (and free) way to co-browse Web pages with users and were heralding it as a technology that, when paired with IM software, could equal the expensive Web-based chat software provided by *QuestionPoint, Tutor.com* and *Docutek*; by 2007, though, the service had shut down (Abram 2005, Francoeur 2005, Pival 2007, Stephens 2005). It is fortunate that no libraries were relying on *Jybe* during its short existence.

With all the excitement over developments taking place on the Web, it is important not to overlook mobile technologies that will likely shape chat reference services in the future. It is now common for cell phones to be enabled to browse the Web, send text messages, and store and play music and video files. Smart phones, such as the Palm *Treo*, BlackBerry *Curve*, and the Apple *iPhone*, grow more popular every year. Also on the horizon are ultramobile PCs (UMPCs), which are essentially supercompact notebook computers that are about the size of a paperback book. Designing Web services for these mobile devices is an area of activity that will only increase as cell phones and wireless devices grow more sophisticated. *Facebook* already has a version optimized for mobile devices. In the coming years, students will not be the only ones who use these advanced devices to connect to library chat services; librarians, too, will increasingly use them. For example, at the library at the University of California, Merced, Michelle Jacobs regularly assists students by using her smart phone to chat, text message, and speak with them while also using the device to search the Web for resources (Jacobs 2007).

As E-mail Fades, Instant Messaging Rises

The current revival of interest in IM software for chat reference services is unlikely to wane in the near future for a number of reasons. Some of these reasons have been valid since the late 1990s, when a number of the earliest chat reference services selected IM over other chat technologies. The strongest arguments for using IM have been that the software is free, stable, easy to learn, and that many students are already using it to communicate with their friends and family. This last point is notable. The number of daily IM users has been steadily rising over the years. In a survey conducted in 2000, sixteen percent of eighteen to twenty-nine year-olds reported having sent an instant message the day before (Pew Internet and American Life Project 2007) By 2006, IM usage was up to sixty-six percent (Lenhart and Madden 2006). An earlier study of technology use by teenagers noted that seventy-five percent of teens who go online use IM, and that among all teens, online or not, two-thirds use IM (Lenhart, Madden, and Hitlin 2005). This study also noted that "when asked about which modes of communication they use most often when communicating with friends, online teens consistently choose IM over e-mail in a wide array of contexts" and "they view e-mail as something you use to talk to 'old people,' institutions, or to send complex instructions to large groups" (ii). Many librarians recognize that by offering IM as a reference communication channel, they are providing students with an interface that is familiar and may reduce the anxiety that some students feel about asking a question. It is not just the incoming waves of students at universities who view IM as a familiar way of communicating; newly minted librarians from this generational cohort are likely to share this preference for IM over e-mail.

Another notable aspect of IM is that users can add others to their buddy lists. Scanning your buddy list allows you to see who is online and whether they are available to chat. This functionality is referred to as "presence," and is an important concept not just in IM but also in social networking sites like *Facebook* and *MySpace*. This desire to display your presence and to keep tabs on the presence of your friends brings to mind Rettig's ideas about the "Net Generation's" use of reference services (a term borrowed from Don Tapscott's book, *Growing Up Digital*). Drawing on Tapscott's generalizations about the Net Generation, Rettig argues that they value "immediacy, interactivity, personalization, and mobility" (2003, 19). In thinking about the "presence functionality" of IM, Rettig links it to the Net Generation's need for immediacy. I agree, and would also argue that the ability to add buddies in your IM client and see if they are online is congruent with the Net Generation's inclinations. Building a buddy list creates a personalized communication galaxy with the user at the center and the handpicked buddies orbiting around. Librarians who launch an IM reference service are creating IM screen names that can be added to buddy lists and thus tap into the drive to personalize that is so prevalent among the Net Generation.

In his vision of the future of reference, Rettig also suggests that we need to move away from seeing reference as always tied to a place, specifically, the reference desk (18). The library Web site, too, is a place, one that the student must visit to get remote reference services. But if a library has an IM reference service, the student who has added the library's screen name to his or her instant messaging buddy list can connect to reference without having to come to a place (the physical library or the virtual library on the Web). Just as librarians could be setting up profiles in *Facebook* and forming a reference cloud outside of our traditional place (the library), we could do the same by offering IM screen names for our students to add to their buddy lists.

In the past five years, companies have spent considerable energy on expanding the realm of the possible with IM software. While in the 1990s, IM messaging meant using one company's software client to chat with your friends using the same client (AOL users could only chat with other AOL users, etc.), there has been some movement toward interoperability between clients. Furthermore, as mentioned earlier, there are now services such as *Trillian*, *Meebo*, and *Pidgin*, that allow you to monitor screen names from different commercial IM services in one place. If you use Google's *Gmail* service, you can now use a Web interface initially designed for e-mail to chat with other *Gmail* users who are in your contact list.

The leading commercial IM clients have also begun offering much more than messaging features, such as advanced technologies like VoIP, file sharing, and video conferencing. Some libraries have begun to use the commercial IM client interface so they can offer these additional modes of communication. For example, Queensland University of Technology uses the *Windows Live Messenger* client so that it can use IM and VoIP with students, and Ohio University has begun using *Skype* for the IM, VoIP, and video conferencing that it offers.

As some of the major commercial IM services continue to exclude one another from their networks, a movement to use an open IM protocol known as *Jabber* has been gaining momentum. Also known as XMPP, for extensible messaging and presence protocol, *Jabber* allows anyone to set up a server with *Jabber* and run their own IM service. Google has done this with their *GTalk* service, but remains alone among the major IM services to have adopted *Jabber*. One of the key advantages of using *Jabber* is that it gives you control over the server where archives of the IM sessions are stored. The commercial IM services detail user privacy in their terms of service documents, but none of them allow librarians to have any sort of control over those archives.

It is worth stressing, though, that just because there is great value in offering reference service via instant messaging, does not mean that librarians should abandon Web-based chat software as an option. There does not have to be an either/or choice between IM and Web-based chat software; it can be a both/and proposition instead. Research into who uses IM reference services and Web-based chat reference services suggests that they are reaching different audiences and that they are used for different purposes.

One study, comparing the use of a college library's IM reference to its Web-based chat service, found that because one part of the college population (the undergraduates) clearly preferred IM, while others (the graduate students and faculty) leaned toward the Web-based service, it was advisable for the library to continue to maintain both (Ward and Kern 2006). This study also shed light on the different ways that IM and Web-based chat are used by patrons. Librarians staffing the two services noticed that users of the IM service tended to "get part of an answer to a question…and then do some research on their own and return to IM once they have a question on the next step of the process," a pattern not apparent in the way the Web-based chat service was used (426). Running two parallel chat services (an IM one and a Web-based one that uses more complex software) may be a good way, then, to meet different needs and different users. It might also be useful for answering different kinds of questions; academic libraries that offer an IM-based service as well as a Web-based chat service have reported that their IM service seems to be best for handling questions that are local in nature (such as what the fine is for overdue books) or are easy to answer (such as ready reference questions) and their Web-based chat service is better poised for dealing with in-depth, research questions (King 2007; Lupien and Rourke 2007).

It is worth noting, though, that despite the increasing interest in IM software for chat services, there are some oft-mentioned objections to the software that are unlikely to be resolved in the near future. The biggest flaw with IM software is that presently there is no way for more than one librarian to be logged in to a screen name at a time. If the library at State College, for example, sees demand for the service grow to the point where the librarian online is juggling several patrons at the same time, it is not possible to simply have a second librarian log in to the same screen name and pick up the additional traffic. Since only one librarian can monitor the service at a time, it is not feasible to build a large-scale collaborative chat service where dozens of librarians can be online simultaneously and respond to chats from patrons at member libraries (there are, though, some interesting projects in development that might allow multiple librarian logins in an IM-based service, which will be discussed a bit later). Web-based chat software, which was built for the needs of online call centers where dozens of operators might be online to chat with e-commerce customers, does not suffer from the scalability flaw that IM does.

Another problem with IM software in library chat services is that, unless the library is running its own IM server, the transcripts are not exclusively stored on servers under the library's control. Those transcripts remain on the servers of the companies who are providing the service: AOL, Yahoo!, etc. As Minow and Neuhaus note, "information stored on a third party site (vendor) likely has less legal protection than information stored on a library's server" (2005, 12). None of the major IM software providers has shown any sign of allowing users to access their transcripts, let alone edit them to remove personal information or delete them altogether. Web-based chat software, though, often allows librarians to have far greater control over the storage of transcripts, even if the transcripts are stored on external servers.

Librarians who want full control over the transcripts of chat sessions generated in an IM service do have a choice, which is to set up an IM server on their own network. This can be done in two ways. First, a library could install open-source server software that uses *Jabber*. Second, one could purchase proprietary enterprise IM server software, which is popular with corporations that need to exercise complete control over the messages that their employees send. In the next five years, it is likely that people who use commercial IM clients from AOL, Yahoo!, and Microsoft will be able to successfully send their messages through *Jabber* servers and enterprise IM servers. In short, interoperability among IM clients should continue to improve in the future.

An unresolved legal question related to commercial IM services is likely to linger in the future. It has been noted that librarians who use commercial IM accounts for reference service might be violating the terms of service agreements from those IM providers, which state that their services are for personal use only (Lankes 2007; Tucker-Raymond 2007b). No library has yet had their chat service shut down because of this, but it remains an unresolved issue. While it may seem farfetched that companies as large and busy as AOL or Microsoft might take legal action against libraries for misusing their IM software, it is worth recalling how *Facebook* shut down profile pages of libraries in 2006 because they were violating the terms of service that, at the time, limited profiles to individuals.

Co-browsing Will Continue to Bedevil Librarians

One of the early strengths of Web-based chat software was that it allowed librarians to take control of the patron's browser and navigate Web sites and subscription databases in ways that might actually teach the patron something. The promise of synching the browsers of patron and librarian, called co-browsing, has been half-fulfilled. The biggest barrier has been system incompatibility. Co-browsing has been limited to situations where both the librarian and patron are using the Internet Explorer browser on a Windows machine (some other browser-operating system combinations may allow one way page pushing). There are no signs that this limitation will be solved in the near future.

As noted by Lupien (2006), co-browsing technology has also been stymied by patrons' firewalls and pop-up blockers. Authentication systems and proxy servers used by libraries have also been known to interfere with co-browsing. Despite the obvious benefits that co-browsing offers for instruction in reference interactions, librarians often become so frustrated by technological problems that they are unwilling to use it in chat sessions (Graves and Desai 2006).

The Number and Size of Collaborative Reference Services Will Keep Growing

The earliest chat reference services were all run as stand-alone services. It did not take long, however, for libraries to begin to recognize the efficiency of working together and sharing a collaborative service. According to Susan McGlamery (in a 2007 conversation with the author) the largest collaborative service, *QuestionPoint*, had nearly a thousand libraries in its public library cooperative service and close to three hundred in the academic cooperative as of July 2007. Many collaborations were formed when individual libraries running their own services struggled to meet demand, which often came in the form of several or more patrons logging in at the same time to chat, or in the form of patrons trying to get help during hours when the library was closed. It is worth noting that the demand often continues after the collaborative is established; statewide collaborative services have found use rising (Hirko 2005). This growth was made possible by the use of Web-based chat software, which was designed to allow large numbers of librarians to be logged on simultaneously and to permit patron queuing, routing, and transferring.

Collaborative chat services offer a number of benefits over standalone chat services. First, the price of subscribing to Web-based chat software is lowered. At Baruch College, our subscription price to *QuestionPoint* went down by sixty percent once we went from being solo subscribers to group subscribers with three other colleges in the City University of New York (CUNY) system. With every additional CUNY college that joins the group, our individual subscription costs decline further. Other library groups have reported similar savings (Bailey-Hainer 2005; Bishop and Torrence 2006). Second, patrons can gain access to a wider range of libraries that may be able to help them. A difficult question or one requiring resources unique to a library other than the patron's local library can often be transferred live or passed along for followup via e-mail. Collaboration provides a way for libraries "to leverage our greatest asset, staff" (Tucker-Raymond 2007a). Third, collaborative services allow libraries to support expanded service hours (in many cases, to a 24/7/365 schedule).

There is a great (and mostly unrealized) desire among librarians to figure out a way to use IM software to power a collaborative chat service. There are some efforts underway that challenge long-held assumptions about the use of IM software for chat reference. The AskNow service that operates in Australia and New Zealand had been using the *QuestionPoint* software for a number of years to run a collaborative reference service. As described by Davis (2007), AskNow launched a pilot project in November 2006 using IM software to run a parallel chat service staffed by librarians from member libraries in the cooperative. Librarians from the institutions took turns, one-at-a-time, logging in to an IM bundling service

(*Gaim*) to monitor screen names set up for the service in each of the leading IM systems (Yahoo!, AIM, etc.).

Despite the popularity of the service with both patrons and the librarians staffing it, it was recognized that it would not scale well as demand grew and the number of simultaneous chat sessions increased. The administrators of the pilot then began developing a customized *Jabber* server that would offer much of the functionality found in Web-based chat software: multiple librarians logged in and monitoring; systems for routing and queuing patrons; local storage of transcripts; and robust reporting and statistics. Once this custom-built system is completed and working, other libraries can adapt the technology for their own cooperative services. The caveat about such an approach, though, is that software development and maintenance are no longer handled by a vendor but by the library coopera-tive. There have been other notable efforts to explore the limits of IM software for reference services. The statewide chat service in Oregon, *L-net*, used eighteen librarians to test enterprise IM software in 2007 to see how well it would work in a collaborative setting and to find out what librarians and patrons thought of the IM service (Tucker-Raymond 2007c). At the University of North Carolina at Chapel Hill, the librarians are exploring a modification of the IM bundling software from *Pidgin* to see if multiple logins for a screen name might be possible (Furuta 2007).

Chat Transcripts Mined More Frequently

A final set of predictions about the future of chat reference relates to the growing mountain of session transcripts that librarians are compiling. The uses to which those transcripts will be put will grow more varied and refined. Transcripts are now commonly used for training staff, quality control review, evaluating librarian performance, building searchable knowledge bases, and providing data for research projects. The statewide chat cooperative service in Oregon, *L-net*, has experimented over the years with a number of projects that repurpose session transcripts. They are used to generate "buzz reports" about what is being asked; to find which Web sites users are being referred to most often; and to plot patron locations using zip codes provided at log in. As a way of demonstrating to would-be users of the service what a chat session looks like on *L-net*, the Web site offers a way to watch a replay of a real chat session. The screen shows the user's chat interface and displays in screencast-like fashion the librarian and patron exchanging messages. The messages all come from an actual chat session that took place on the *L-net* service and has since been scrubbed of personal information so it can be publicly viewed.

For a fascinating vision of the future of chat, the Stella chatbot on the State and University Library Hamburg Web site offers a lively preview. Sitting atop what appears to be an IM interface on the Web site is an animated avatar named Stella, whose facial expressions change as she "replies" to your typed questions. She offers basic advice about resources and services at the library as well as links to relevant pages on the library Web site. Examining this chatbot service more closely, one can see that the user's "questions" or "messages" are automatically queried against a knowledge base that the library has created (Christensen 2006). Although Stella might appear to be chatting with you, she is simply presenting the single best search result to your natural language query of the Stella's knowledge base. Stella's animations are carefully calibrated to the specific message she returns to you and employ sophisticated technology from *Novomind*, a company that sells this animated avatar software mostly to online merchants.

While many libraries offer searchable knowledge bases built from the bits and pieces of previous digital reference interactions, they usually present a simple search box as the interface. Instead, Stella offers a knowledge base interface that mimics IM software and that may be more enjoyable for patrons to interact with. While it is not likely that library chat reference services will be replaced with chatbots, it might be interesting to use a chatbot as the means by which users query a knowledge base of prior chat session transcripts.

Conclusion

It is clear that the means of communicating via the Web will continue to expand and diversify. Not only will we see new tools, but we will find many of those tools are interoperable. Other tools will become embedded in social networks or actually be social networks (like *Facebook*). As mobile phone technology grows more sophisticated and integrated into the Web, there will be a blurring of the line between Web communication tools and mobile communication. All of these developments will offer librarians more opportunities and challenges for providing chat reference service. Our communication tools will more and more become multi-channel services similar to *Skype*, which can be used for IM, VoIP, and video reference services. The debates over IM versus Web-based chat software will diminish as the technologies advance and converge, and the need to choose one or the other is eliminated; instead, librarians will have a panoply of options, all of which will make it easier for them to go where their users are.

Sources for Additional Research

Davis, K. 2007. AskNow instant messaging: Innovation in virtual reference. http://www.nla.gov.au/nla/staffpaper/2007/documents/IM-ALJ-article.pdf.
> Davis describes how the nationwide chat service in Australia, which had long used the *QuestionPoint* software for its collaborative staffing, successfully demonstrated the viability of running a cooperative service based on IM software.

Forster, S. 2005. Instant messaging and online reference: An Altarama white paper. North Orem, UT: Altarama Information Systems.
> This essay summarizes the main arguments for using IM software for chat and its relative advantages over Web-based chat software.

Horowitz, L. R., Patricia A. Flanagan, and D. L. Helman. 2005. The viability of live online reference: An assessment. *portal: Libraries and the Academy* 5 (2): 239-58.
> This publication details a project that did not meet expectations and was discontinued. The authors present their findings from the assessment of the Web-based chat reference

service at the Massachusetts Institute of Technology and thoughtfully elaborate which parts of their library's service did not meet their or their user's expectations.

Houghton, S., and A. Schmidt. 2005. Web-based chat vs. instant messaging: Who wins? *Online* 29 (4): 26-30.
> The authors compare reference services powered by IM to those that use Web-based chat software in ten areas: speed, cost, availability of librarians, training, user base, software, features, computer requirements, privacy, and community. The authors recommend IM software.

Lupien, P. 2006. Virtual reference in the age of pop-up blockers, firewalls, and Service Pack 2. *Online* 30 (4): 14-19. http://www.infotoday.com/online/jul06/Lupien.shtml.
> Lupien explains in detail how Web-based chat software is increasingly hobbled by improving security technology on the computers of our users.

Radford, M. L., and M. K. Kern. 2006. A multiple-case study of the discontinuation of nine chat reference services. *Library & Information Science Research* 28 (4): 521-47.
> In this article the authors identify a number of common themes that emerged through data collection which was accomplished via interviews, questionnaires, and analysis of internal documents from the libraries studied. Most salient were the reasons why the libraries decided to end chat service.

Sloan, B. 2006. Twenty years of chat reference. *Internet Reference Services Quarterly* 11 (2): 91-95.
> This thumbnail sketch of how libraries have used various technologies to chat online with patrons serves as the standard account of the history of chat reference. It is particularly valuable for an account of the earliest services, some of which are now long gone.

Ward, D. and M. K. Kern. 2006. Combining IM and vendor-based chat: A report from the frontlines of an integrated service. *portal: Libraries and the Academy* 6 (4): 417-429.
> The authors present a study of what it was like at the University of Illinois at Urbana-Champaign to run an IM service using *Trillian* alongside a Web-based chat reference service (which used Docutek's *VRLplus* software). Despite the comparatively greater popularity of the IM service, the authors recommend keeping both systems running to meet the needs of different user groups on campus.

Works Cited

Abram, S. 2005. Three ways to understand professional grade virtual reference. *Information Outlook* 9: 34-35.

Bailey-Hainer, B. 2005. Virtual reference: Alive and well. *Library Journal* 130 (1): 46-47.

Bishop, B. W., and M. Torrence. 2006. Virtual reference services: Consortium vs. stand-alone. *College & Undergraduate Libraries* 13 (4): 117-27.

boyd, d. Forthcoming. Why youth (heart) social network sites: The role of networked publics in teenage social life. In *Youth, Identity, and Digital Media,* ed. David Buckingham.

Chat reference libraries. *LISWiki*. http://liswiki.org/wiki/Chat_reference_libraries.

Chapman, S. 2007. Facebook users prefer in-person librarian interactions. *Userslib.com*. http://userslib.com/?p=74.

Christensen, A. 2006. Stella: Library chatbots in electronic reference. Slide presentation at the annual Access Conference, Ottawa, ON, Canada.

Coffman, S, and L. Arret. 2004a. To chat or not to chat: Taking another look at virtual reference, part 1. *Searcher* 12 (July/August): 38-46.

Coffman, S., and L. Arret. 2004b. To chat or not to chat: Taking yet another look at virtual reference, part 2. *Searcher* 12 (September): 49-56.

Davis, K. 2007. AskNow instant messaging: Innovation in virtual reference. http://www.nla.gov.au/nla/staffpaper/2007/documents/IM-ALJ-article.pdf.

Forster, S. 2005. Instant messaging and online reference: An Altarama white paper. North Orem, Utah: Altarama Information Systems.

Francoeur, S. 2001. An analytical review of chat reference services. *Reference Services Review* 29 (3): 189-203.

Francoeur, S. 2005. Jybe ho! *Digital Reference.* http://www.teachinglibrarian.org/weblog/2005/04/jybe-ho.html.

Furuta, K. Instant messaging and collaborative virtual reference. Slide presentation at the Collaborative Virtual Reference Symposium, Denver, CO. http://www.coloradovirtuallibrary.org/reference/2007VRSymposium/Kenneth_Furuta.pdf

Graves, S. J., and C. M. Desai. 2006. Instruction via chat reference: Does co-browse help? *Reference Services Review* 34 (3): 340-357.

Hirko, B. 2005. Mainstreaming chat. *Library Journal NetConnect* 130: 32.

Horowitz, L. R., P. A. Flanagan, and Deborah L. Helman. 2005. The viability of live online reference: An assessment. *portal: Libraries and the Academy* 5 (2): 239-58.

Houghton, S., and A. Schmidt. 2005. Web-based chat vs. instant messaging: who wins? *Online* 29 (4): 26-30.

Jacobs, M. 2007. acrl2007 Cyber Zed Shed: Make your services smarter: How smartphones can extend your service and let you work away from your office and the reference desk. http://michelleljacobs.googlepages.com/acrl2007.

King, V. 2007. Acting globally, acting locally: Local instant messaging and collaborative VR. Slide presentation at the Collaborative Virtual Reference Symposium, Denver, CO. http://www.coloradovirtuallibrary.org/reference/2007VRSymposium/Valery_King.ppt.

Lankes, R. D. 2007. Collecting conversations in a massive scale world. Presentation at the annual meeting of the Association for Library Collections and Technical Services, Washington, D.C. http://quartz.syr.edu/rdlankes/blog/?p=239.

Lenhart, A. and M. Madden. 2006. Generations online. Pew Internet & American Life Project. http://www.pewinternet.org/pdfs/PIP_Generations_Memo.pdf.

Lenhart, A., M. Madden, and P. Hitlin. 2005. Teens and technology. Pew Internet & American Life Project. http://www.pewinternet.org/pdfs/PIP_Teens_Tech_July2005web.pdf.

Lupien, P. 2006. Virtual reference in the age of pop-up blockers, firewalls, and Service Pack 2. *Online* 30 (4): 14-19. http://www.infotoday.com/online/jul06/Lupien.shtml.

Lupien, P. and L. Rourke. 2007. Learning from chatting: How our VR questions are giving us answers. Presentation at the annual meeting of the Canadian Library Association, St. Johns, Newfoundland, Canada. http://www.cla.ca/conference/2007/presentations/Learning%20from%20chatting_%20how%20our%20VR%20questions%20are%20giving%20us%20answers%202007.pdf.

McCulley, L., and O. Reinauer. 2006. Connecting with AIM: The search for a virtual reference niche. *College & Undergraduate Libraries* 13 (4): 43-54.

Minow, M., and P. Neuhaus. 2005. Working paper: Is privacy working? Planning for stronger privacy measures than security through obscurity in library virtual reference services. Paper presented at the Digital Reference and Legal Issues preconference at the annual meeting of the American Library Association, Chicago, Ill. http://www. ala.org/ala/washoff/contactwo/oitp/MinowNeuhaus2005Sept15.pdf.

Morville, P. 2005. *Ambient findability*. Sebastopol, CA.: O'Reilly.

Online reference. *Library Success*. http://www.libsuccess.org/index.php?title=Online_Reference.

Pew Internet and American Life Project. 2007. Usage over time. http://www.pewinternet. org/trends/UsageOverTime.xls.

Pival, P. 2007. Co-browsing tools and technology: A mini-guide. *The Distant Librarian*. http://distlib.blogs.com/distlib/2007/03/cobrowsing_tool.html.

Pogue, D. 2007. Are U.S. cellphone carriers calcified? *Pogue's Posts*. http://pogue.blogs. nytimes.com/2007/07/05/are-us-cellphone-carriers-calcified/.

Pulliam, B. R., and Susan McMullen. 2006. RYT: Are you there? A consortium's switch to IM reference. *College & Undergraduate Libraries* 13 (4): 55-73.

Radford, M. L., and M. K. Kern. 2006. A multiple-case study of the discontinuation of nine chat reference services. *Library & Information Science Research* 28 (4): 521-47.

Rettig, J. 2003. Technology, cluelessness, anthropology, and the memex: The future of academic reference services. *Reference Services Review* 31 (1): 17-21.

Sloan, B. 2006. Twenty years of chat reference. *Internet Reference Services Quarterly* 11: 91-95.

Stephens, M. 2005. Jybe 2.0 is here (RIP VR). *Tame the Web*. http://www.tametheweb. com/ttwblog/archives/001266.html.

Stephens, M. 2006. IM=FASTER virtual reference on the cheap. *Computers in Libraries* 26 (4): 36-37.

Tenopir, C. 2004. Rethinking virtual reference. *Library Journal* (November 1): 34.

Tucker-Raymond, C. 2007a. Collaborative enterprise instant messaging at ALA Midwinter—Part 1, background. *L-net Blog*. http://www.oregonlibraries.net/staff/2007/01/25/ collaborative_enterprise_instant_messaging_at_ala_midwinter.

Tucker-Raymond, C. 2007b. Does IM reference violate terms of service agreements of commercial instant messaging services? *L-net Blog*. http://www.oregonlibraries.net/ staff/2007/07/12/does_im_reference_violate_terms_of_service_agreements_of_commercial_instant_messaging_services.

Tucker-Raymond, C. (2007c) Report on last month's test of alternative software to QuestionPoint. *L-net Blog*. http://www.oregonlibraries.net/staff/2007/09/06/report_on_last_months_test_of_alternative_software_to_questionpoint.

Ward, D. and M. K. Kern. 2006. Combining IM and vendor-based chat: a report from the frontlines of an integrated service. *portal: Libraries and the Academy* 6 (4): 417-429.

CHAPTER 7

Friending our Users: Social Networking and Reference Services

Cliff Landis

Introduction

Social networking sites are changing the way that libraries engage their users. Sometimes called "social networking software" or "social networking services," these Web sites are designed to let users share their lives with friends, family, and the general public. Many librarians immediately saw the possibilities in the proliferating social networks—by connecting with our users in "their space," we are making ourselves readily available and removing many of the obstacles to their information needs.

As reference librarians, our first reaction to new technology is to "set up desk"—to provide the same services we have traditionally offered, only in a new medium. However, new technologies demand a new approach, and recent years have seen librarians offering reference, instruction, and other services in unique and innovative ways.

What is it?

Social networking sites allow users to interact with each other in three different ways. First, a user creates a profile that will represent him or her to other users. This profile is a Web page that includes elements such as demographic information, hobbies, and interests (such as favorite bands, movies, books, and TV programs). Second, social networking sites allow users to interact with each other by sharing media such as videos, photos, music, and Web sites. Third, social networking sites allow users to communicate with each other using public messages, private messages, and blogs. Social networking sites have become powerful social tools because users can quickly identify individuals with similar interests, share media with friends, and directly communicate with other users all in the same Web site.

The "networking" part of social networking sites happens with the action of "Friending." To Friend someone (verb form capitalized for the sake of clarity) means to add that person to your list of Friends so that your two profiles are connected. This connection shows that you belong to each others' social networks. It does not, however, imply that you are actually friends with that person in daily life—Friending is simply a way to publicly display that you are in some way connected to a person for any number of reasons (Donath and boyd 2004, 71). danah boyd, speaking about the social networking site *Friendster*, shows that users are aware that there is a difference between friends and Friends: "Overheard conversations might include statements such as 'She's not my friend, but she's my Friendster' and 'Did you see that Alex is Drew's Friendster? (boyd 2004). By Friending an individual (such as a local librarian) or organization (such as the local library), the user is creating a connection that can be seen by others.

The History and Power Behind Social Networking Sites

The first social networking site was *SixDegrees.com*, which began in 1997 and closed four years later (Donath and boyd 2004). Many social networking sites followed, including *Friendster, Hi5, Bebo, Orkut*, and, of course, the now-ubiquitous *MySpace* and *Facebook. Facebook* will be the primary discussion point of this piece, but many others have proliferated, often setting themselves apart by specializing in different areas such as business relationships (*Ryze, LinkedIn*), school relationships (*Classmates.com, Graduates.com*), and hobbies (*Catster, CarDomain, Sportsvite*). Profiles can also be seen beyond social networking sites, since many popular Web sites give users the option to create profiles and connections with other users (*LiveJournal, YouTube, Xanga, LibraryThing, Flickr*).

The more users a social networking site has, the more powerful a tool it is to connect with other people. A large social network allows users to stay in touch with individuals throughout their lives. According to Dunbar's Rule of 150, we have the ability to mentally maintain relationships with approximately 147.8 individuals—this number is conventionally rounded to 150 (Dunbar 1993, 682). As we meet new friends, we lose contact with some old friends. Social networking sites allow us to maintain contact with those individuals (such as a best friend from middle school). Although the user may not talk to his or her middle school best friends anymore, by Friending them, the user maintains a connection and can still visit their profiles and see where they are and what they are doing.

Social networking Web sites are changing the Internet as a whole. As of May 14, 2007, five of the top twenty-five most visited Web sites were social networking sites (*MySpace, Orkut, Hi5, Facebook* and *Friendster*, in that order), and many of the other top twenty-five had the ability to create and connect profiles (Alexa.com 2007). Users look to each other for information, and social networking sites help to make that communication possible. People make use of social networking sites' built-in and user-designed applications to discover new music, plan parties, catch up on gossip, find interesting events to attend, watch TV shows, and creatively express themselves through blogs, videos, quizzes and comments.

The differences between social networking sites are important to note. Some, such as *MySpace*, allow users to create both personal and institutional profiles. This flexibility allows librarians to represent the library, the Reference Services department, or just themselves. *MySpace* also gives users the ability to edit the overall appearance and organization of the page, allowing you to brand your profile appropriately. Other sites, such as *Facebook*, limit profiles to individuals and do not allow editing of the profile's appearance. Instead, *Facebook* allows institutions to create "Pages," which give some of the functionality of profiles (such as the ability to send messages and comment). In addition, a Page creator can monitor how many times the Page has been viewed and create advertisement campaigns. Although the inability to create institutional profiles may seem like a drawback to *Facebook*'s service, it emphasizes the personal social network, and also gives users the benefit of a consistent interface. Additionally,

Facebook allows the addition of user-created applications. Some are relevant to librarian profiles, such as library catalog and polling applications; others, such as "(fluff) Friends" and "My Aquarium" are primarily for entertainment and can unnecessarily clutter a librarian's profile. Similarly, Google has created *OpenSocial*, a user-created application set that would allow the sharing of applications between social networks like *Orkut, MySpace, Friendster* and others. This would prove particularly beneficial for libraries that would want to spread their catalog search interfaces into social networking sites. The differences in social networking sites should be taken into account as you develop your (or your library's) profiles.

Reservations

As with any new technology, many librarians have reservations about the place that social networking sites should have in the library. These reservations are partially due to negative media portrayals in recent years. There is also the perception that libraries are moving away from their mission of delivering information, and are instead turning into community playgrounds. Before I move on to the role of social networking sites in reference service, I would like to address these and other concerns.

Privacy, Predators, and Freedom of Information

Librarians have long stood at the forefront on the battle for privacy rights, so it is not surprising that librarians are skeptical of social networking sites, which connect people through the disclosure of personal information. Yet, librarians are not alone in their concerns about privacy; social networking site users are concerned, too. In September 2006, *Facebook* launched its "mini-feed feature," which aggregated all of a user's behavior on *Facebook* and put it into an RSS (Really Simple Syndication) feed on their friends' homepages—making all a user's actions (from adding friends to changing relationship status) visible to everyone they listed as a friend. There was an immediate backlash, including a barrage of complaints, a petition, and the creation of a protest Web site (Cashmore 2006a). *Facebook* responded by creating a "My Privacy" feature, which greatly enhanced users' ability to control what information was visible to other users. This reaction was a surprise for social networking sites, which discovered that their users are quite aware of the privacy implications of their behavior, and are willing to fight to protect their privacy.

MySpace and *Facebook* gained negative attention when the media highlighted. instances of sexual predation on social networking sites. However, Larry Rosen studied over 1,400 teenaged *MySpace* users to determine the instances of predation, with the following results:

> First…stalking is extremely rare, happening about 1.3% of the time, while being approached for sex happens slightly more often, roughly 5.1% of the time. Second, given the explanations from MySpacers, it

appears that, for the vast majority, the episode [of being approached for sex] was brushed off and had no lasting impact. (Rosen 2006)

Most teens and adults who use social networking sites are savvy when it comes to blocking communications from sexual predators. Unfortunately, governments respond to the fears drummed up by media reports by legislating blocks against social networking sites from libraries and schools, rather than by educating students on appropriate and safe ways to use them. This restriction of access to information does not stop students who use social networking sites from home, but instead further limits the opportunities for students who access these sites from schools or libraries for educational purposes.

But It's Kid Stuff!

Many librarians see these Web sites as inappropriate for educational institutions or faculty. There is still a perception that *MySpace* is geared toward high-school students, and is therefore inappropriate for colleges and universities. However, according to a comScore report in October 2006, "Internet users between the ages of 35-54 now account for 40.6 percent of the MySpace visitor base, an 8.2 percentage point increase during the past year" (comScore 2006). Individuals of all kinds are using *MySpace* to connect with friends.

In 2006, *Facebook* opened to non-students. There were initial fears that it would lose its core of college and university students as members of the public joined the site. However, as Pete Cashmore predicted, since *Facebook* opened their service to the public, there has not been an "exodus of Facebook users" (Cashmore, 2006b). The future will show whether *Facebook's* demographic eventually grows beyond the college crowd, but for now *Facebook* is an excellent way to reach academic library users.

Who Can Keep Up?

Some librarians have commented that social networking sites are just "one more thing" to add to the list of things to keep up with, and that they fall outside of our mission—to deliver information and instruction to library users. Admittedly, in the realm of reference services, things are changing almost daily—as they always have been. The library profession has a history of working with the latest technology to help users, whether through punch cards or instant messaging, microfilm or databases. We have always struggled to keep abreast of these changes, and now have new tools (such as blogs and RSS) to stay up-to-date with these changes.

We now have to compete with services such as Yahoo! Answers and search engines such as Google. For libraries to stay relevant in this new information environment, we must provide excellent service—service that our users cannot get elsewhere. The key is to discover both what users *want* and what users *need*—and then supply *both*. Social networking sites can be a great way to discover these wants and needs, because they can be used for marketing, reference, instruction, and improvement of services.

Current Uses
Library Marketing

Library marketing often falls to reference and instruction librarians, since they provide the in-depth human resources that students, faculty and staff turn to for research help. Yet, most librarians can relate an experience in which library users complain about the library lacking a particular service or resource, when in fact the resource was there, but unknown. This type of complaint shows where library marketing is valuable:

> Libraries have a long tradition of bringing services wherever their patrons are located, through such approaches as bookmobiles and branches in strip malls and community centers. This has also become the case in the online world. While most libraries have their own Web sites, some are also starting to push their services to the online sites at which patrons congregate. (Farkas 2007, 27)

Social networking sites are the next generation of word-of-mouth marketing. An example is the University of Illinois at Urbana-Champaign's (UIUC) Undergraduate Library's *MySpace* page (http://www.myspace.com/undergradlibrary). The library has over four hundred Friends, including students, local bands, and other library-related users. Changes in hours, events and new services are advertised via *MySpace's* blogging tool, while a catalog search box has been embedded into the "About Me" section. Additionally, the UIUC Undergraduate Library has created a *Facebook* profile and joined other libraries in creating *Facebook* applications which allow users to add a catalog search box on their profiles (http://apps.facebook.com/uiuclibrary/). Each of these efforts increases the library's online visibility.

Marketing using social networking sites can be a time- and budget-saving way to reach out to library users. As Judith A. Seiss explains in *The Visible Librarian*, "If you're wondering when to market, the answer is easy—always. Every encounter with a customer or a prospective customer is a marketing opportunity" (2003, 33). Social networking sites can reach users whenever they log on through an interface they are already familiar with. This can be more inviting than library Web sites which are (too often) hierarchical and difficult to navigate.

Social networking sites are also a free way to reach out to potential library users. By performing advanced searches, you can discover individuals at your institution who list "books" or "reading" as one of their interests, or if your employees are thinking of setting up a gaming night at your library, a search for "gaming" as an interest will provide you with a quick invitation list. Create an event and users will be able to confirm whether they are attending. Do you have a marketing budget? Consider purchasing "flyers" on *Facebook*—short advertisements that appear to users at your university. No money? You can still post bulletins on *MySpace* and notes on *Facebook* to let users know about upcoming events.

Whether or not to actively Friend library users is a debatable topic. Millennial students are used to receiving advertisements from corporations and organizations through social networking sites that allow such accounts. Therefore, organizations (such as libraries) can often Friend library users without appearing too assuming. However, individual librarians who actively try to Friend users may be perceived as pushy. So, it may be best to reach out to users through other means, and allow them to Friend you;

> However, this actually works out—students like counting faculty as their friends. If you've created a rich profile, it shows students that you care about Facebook, and use it somewhat regularly. With the advent of news feeds, students will broadcast the fact they've [F]riended you, and this will start the friend requests coming in. (Stutzman 2006)

Regardless of which tools or methods you choose to employ with social networking sites, they should be part of a larger marketing plan. The plan will ensure that information such as blog posts, pictures, and event invitations tie into the larger picture of the library.

Reference

Many of the same tools that can be used for marketing via social networking sites can also be employed to provide more traditional reference services. Messages can be sent directly between users (similar to e-mail), so that direct, private questions can be asked. Public messages can be displayed on the user's profile (called "commenting" on *MySpace*, and "writing on a user's wall" on *Facebook*). Also, groups can be created to give users a forum to ask reference questions. At Valdosta State University, I created an "Ask the Librarian" *Facebook* group. Groups in *Facebook* have both public message space, as well as discussion boards. Students ask questions in both of these forums, which allow other students to see both the questions asked and the answers provided (Landis 2007, 6). Some libraries choose to provide reference services directly within these social networking sites. In these instances, I strongly recommend that librarians make use of any e-mail notification systems provided. These notification systems will alert staff to new questions immediately, so that they will not be forced to log in several times a day to check the social site for new questions. In addition to communication tools provided by the social networking services, some libraries (such as the Public Library of Charlotte & Mecklenburg County—http://myspace.com/libraryloft/) are using plug-ins and widgets to provide chat reference services directly from their profile, allowing users to seek reference help without leaving the page.

The largest risk associated with providing reference services through social networking sites is stretching services too thin. For example, creating in-depth reference discussion boards on several different social networking sites can dilute the service that users receive. An alternative is to set up a knowledge base at your library's Web site, and to allow users to (anonymously) post questions. A link to the knowledge base from each of your online profiles allows users to ask questions and search for answers.

Instruction

In addition to providing reference services via social networking sites, librarians can also provide instruction. In his blog post *Facebook as a Tool for Learning Engagement*, Fred Stutzman offers an introductory caveat regarding instruction in social networking sites:

> Facebook isn't Blackboard or any other course management system. It isn't a wiki, or a blog, or any sort of silver bullet tool. Facebook is the digital social center of the college campus. It is a social tool; its use is primarily the management of the social life at college. Of course, college life is geared around academics, so inherently the social worlds of college students intersect with academics—but only to a certain extent. (Stutzman 2006)

Keeping this information in mind, it should be noted that *Facebook* has been used by students for organizing study groups, and by professors to deploy course content. By making connections with users, librarians can embed themselves into both kinds of groups, offering users the instruction that they require at the point of need.

One of the laments of instruction librarians is that there is never enough time with the students. By mentioning your profile at the beginning and end of an instruction session, you can encourage students to contact you if they have any questions. This attention makes an impression on students; although they may discard handouts or neglect to write down an e-mail address, a quick search for "librarian" will reveal your profile. Later, when students have research questions, they can ask for help and receive instruction at the point of need.

For the Other Folks in the Library...

Reference librarians are not the only potential beneficiaries of social networking sites. In the case of library technology, there is often a disconnect between the "front end" services and "back end" services of libraries—particularly when users want to report a problem or request a service. Social networking sites can often help to reduce this gap. By providing a forum for offering suggestions, the library can reach out to users and improve service.

In *Going Where Patrons Are: Outreach in MySpace and Facebook*, Meredith Farkas tells the story of Bennington (Va.) College's library director Oceana Wilson, who uses her *Facebook* profile to solicit collection development suggestions. As Farkas explains, "Although most libraries have an acquisitions suggestion form, students may not feel comfortable using it or may think the form is only meant for faculty. In this case, Bennington is coming into students' virtual space to say, 'We care about your opinion'" (2007, 27). This outreach is an excellent example of making the effort to remove barriers between users and library services.

Where Libraries are Headed—And How to Get There
Creating your Brand

Also on the topic of marketing, many libraries are looking at the concept of branding—in other words, tying all of a library's advertising efforts under a single memorable theme, slogan or icon. An excellent example is Ann Arbor District Library, whose Web site (http://www.aadl.org/) and *MySpace* profile (http://www. myspace.com/annarbordistrictlibrary) share the same color scheme and font. The *MySpace* page has a younger, funkier feel, but is still recognizable due to the consistency of the branding. When users visit these pages, they know that they are looking at Ann Arbor District Library, regardless of the Web site's URL.

As libraries create brand identity, they separate themselves from other sources of information and define what makes them different and valuable. This identity can then be spread throughout different social networking sites, as well as other Web-based and face-to-face tools (such as IM and Twitter icons, wikis, name tags, flyers, and library signage).

Your Friendly Librarian

Some services do not allow for the creation of institutional profiles (such as *Facebook* and *Hi5*). In these cases, librarians create their own profiles and engage with library users directly. It may seem tempting to create a fake "Marion the Librarian" profile, and to make "her" part of your library's brand, but this goes against the idea of social networking sites, which is to connect with people directly. So what do students really want to see on a librarian's profile?

> First, they want to know a little about you. They want to know some of your favorite books, movies and TV shows. You get no points for loading your profile with pretentious interests—students want to feel connected to you. If you like the Family Guy or Curb Your Enthusiasm[sic], share it. Second, students like pictures…. The key in creating a profile is sharing a little bit of the real you—when you can make these connections with your students, you will engage them. (Stutzman 2006)

The personal profile of a librarian can do more than just stake your library's claim in a social networking site. Reference librarians are familiar with having students identify a particular librarian as "my librarian." The ability to Friend a librarian provides two significant benefits: the potential to reduce library anxiety and the ability to offer users a consistent human resource for research help.

Making the ILS Friendly

Integrated library systems are already changing to allow for more input from users. Libraries such as the Ann Arbor District Library (http://www.aadl.org/), are modifying their catalogs to allow users to write reviews and add tags. Other libraries, such as the University of Washington Libraries (http://www.lib.washington.edu/), are integrating WorldCat into their catalogs with WorldCat Local. At the same time, book lovers have created Web sites such as *LibraryThing*, which allows users to create their own profiles and catalogs and to Friend other users. This social site allows users to share their favorite book lists and receive recommendations for books they might like.

Features like these allow users to add value to the catalog, and improve the overall user experience. These efforts, of course, should always be designed as opt-in, allowing users to protect their right to read and their right to privacy. Yet many individuals are willing to set aside their privacy in order to interact and share in their interests with others.

Keeping up
If you are feeling a bit overwhelmed by all of this, do not worry. Wherever you can dream of going, a librarian is already there. In every social networking site I have joined, there is at least one group page created by librarians, for librarians. If you are curious, search a site for the word "librarians" or "libraries," and you will find your colleagues ready to help!

Conclusion
Social networking sites are taking reference services beyond the traditional reference desk. These sites allow librarians to reach out to users in a familiar interface, and to provide users with instruction, research help and the opportunity to have their voices heard. By joining users in "their space," librarians are able to reduce library anxiety, market their services, and stay connected to what users want and need. All it takes is being a good Friend.

Sources for Additional Research

Casey, M. E., and L. C. Savastinuk. 2007. *Library 2.0: A Guide to Participatory Library Service.* Medford, NJ: Information Today.
> Casey and Savastinuk provide an accessible guide to understanding and implementing an overall Library 2.0 plan. This book includes information on the underlying concepts and values of Library 2.0, technologies to consider (including social networking sites), achieving library-wide buy-in, and how to keep a 2.0 service plan running.

Farkas, M. G. 2007. Social Networking Software. In *Social Software in Libraries,* 109-124. Medford, NJ: Information Today.
> Farkas provides an in-depth look at the origins, history, and variety of social networking sites. She also provides information on doing market research and outreach, and considers privacy and intellectual property implications of using social networking sites.

Library 2.0. http://library20.ning.com/.
> Since its creation, the Library 2.0 network on *Ning* has quickly become a gathering place for librarians using technology to reach and serve library users. Explore this site to get an introduction to everything Library 2.0, and to start collaborating with other librarians.

Mashable: Social Networking News. http://mashable.com/.
Mashable is a community-written blog that carries all the latest news in the world of social networking sites. It is updated several times a day, so use the category tabs (*MySpace, Facebook, YouTube*, etc.) to read only those stories dealing with the social networking sites you are using. RSS feeds are available for each category.

McKiernan, G. 2007. *Friends: Social Networking Sites for Engaged Library Services.* http://onlinesocialnetworks.blogspot.com/.
The *Friends* blog will help you stay up-to-date on how libraries are using social networking sites, and what the media and academe are saying about them.

Schmit, A. 2007. *walking paper.* http://www.walkingpaper.org/.
Aaron Schmit's blog is a great resource for information on Library 2.0 technologies. He has written and presented extensively on libraries' use of *MySpace* and *Facebook*.

Works Cited

Alexa Internet Inc. "Alexa Web Search: Top 500". Alexa the Web Information Company. http://www.alexa.com/site/ds/top_sites?ts_mode=global&lang=none.

Boyd, D. "Friendster and Publicly Articulated Social Networks." Conference on Human Factors and Computing Systems (CHI 2004). Vienna: ACM, April 24-29, 2004.

Cashmore, P. 2006. Facebook Backlash. http://mashable.com/2006/09/06/the-facebook-backlash-begins/.

——— 2006. Facebook Regions Launches. http://mashable.com/2006/09/26/facebook-regions/.

comScore, Inc. "More than Half of MySpace Visitors are Now Age 35 or Older, as the Site's Demographic Composition Continues to Shift". comScore, Inc. http://www.comscore.com/press/release.asp?press=1019.

Donath, J. and d. boyd. 2004. Public displays of connection. *BT Technology Journal* 22 (4): 71-82.

Dunbar, R.I.M. 1993. Coevolution of neocortical size, group size and language in humans. *The Behavioral and Brain Sciences* 16 (4): 681-735.

Farkas, M. 2007. Going Where Patrons Are: Outreach in MySpace and Facebook. *American Libraries* 38: 27.

Landis, C. 2007. Good idea! Connecting to users with Facebook. *Georgia Library Quarterly* 43 (4): 6.

Rosen, L. D. 2006. Sexual Predators on MySpace: A Deeper Look at Teens Being Stalked or Approached for Sexual Liaisons. http://www.csudh.edu/psych/ SEXUAL%20PREDATORS%20ON%20MYSPACE%20Short%20Report%202006-01.pdf.

Siess, J. A. 2003. *Visible Librarian: Asserting Your Value with Marketing and Advocacy.* Chicago: American Library Association.

Stutzman, F. December 20, 2006. Facebook as a tool for Learning Engagement. http://chimprawk.blogspot.com/2006/12/facebook-as-tool-for-learning.html.

CHAPTER 8

Preemptive Reference: Coming out from Behind the Desk

Brian S. Mathews

The first things that often come to mind when people think of libraries are the books. Next is the librarian sitting behind a reference desk wearing glasses with her hair in a bun, casting a suspicious glance at all those who pass. This stereotype is unfortunate, yet it undoubtedly lives on in the popular consciousness. As academic libraries shift to digital collections, so too have our services; much can be done online. The reference desk, a long- standing symbol of our function, is now just one of many avenues from which patrons can receive assistance. This chapter introduces a mindset for moving beyond the desk and striving to be more immersive and interactive with our communities. The Preemptive Approach constitutes a shift to a more proactive rather than passive role for the reference librarian, with the goal of reaching patrons before they would typically consider turning to the library for help, as well as delivering instruction at a point of genuine need.

The Current State of Reference

Not too long ago, library collections were tangible and stored within the building. Books were located using a card catalog, and print indexes helped identify potentially relevant journal articles. Reference collections were stocked abundantly with handbooks, directories, and encyclopedias. This was the environment from which reference was born. With materials gathered in-house, it was ideal to provide assistance in the place where users needed it. However, collections are no longer predominately *accessed* in person. Book and journal searches can be done anywhere at anytime. Web technologies have pushed resources outside of the building's physical boundaries. This shift has also changed the delivery of reference service; the desk is no longer the centerpiece of assistance, but rather, it is just one channel to which users can turn for help.

In recent years, virtual reference and instant messaging have emerged as new methods for bringing service to the patron. A student researching from home, work, a café, or even within the library can easily interact with staff. If our collections are online, then it makes sense that reference assistance should be present as well. These virtual chat tools greatly complement e-mail and telephone services in providing an array of communication options for patrons.

Although librarians continuously strive to become more accessible, we still require action on behalf of the user. A student still needs to approach us, whether at the desk or via text message, in order to initiate contact. Studies indicate that reference transactions have been in gradual decline, so while the patrons who do turn to us for help may be satisfied, the majority of users do not take advantage of our services. The traditional reference process, in which we wait *just in case* the user has a question, is passive; patrons bring us their information problems to be solved. It is not uncommon for students to visit the library the day before an assignment is due and expect librarians to uncover the appropriate resources. This encounter can be frustrating for both parties if the subject area is limited or there is a tight deadline. Despite a plethora of online resources, Web tutorials, and classroom instructional tools, students often need help conducting efficient research. The emergence of the Social Web provides new opportunities to move beyond the "help desk" model and make reference a more ubiquitous experience.

The Preemptive Approach

Can we reach users before they would traditionally consider coming to us for help? This is the core mindset of the Preemptive Approach: seeking better integration with our community instead of expecting users to always go out of their way to access the library. Rather than simply adopting new technologies to continue answering questions, this mindset requires a philosophical shift in how we approach students.

Compared with Web searching, libraries are not very user friendly. Our Web sites are complicated, our database selection is overwhelming, our classification system is complex, and our catalogs are not as easy to search as Amazon's. Although some tools, like federated searching and link resolvers, have improved functionality, libraries are not the first place that students turn to for their information needs (De Rosa 2005). Research anxiety is very common—libraries are confusing and intimidating, with even advanced users struggling to locate resources. This perception of libraries being complicated or too difficult makes them less desirable for research needs, especially compared with the ease of Web searching. In many case, libraries are the place that students turn to as a last resort.

The Preemptive Approach aims to take the library outside of these preconceived boundaries and to be more immersive within the patron's daily life. Instead of a wait-and-see attitude, this process embraces an entrepreneurial outlook by seeking a more opportunistic delivery of library services and resources. Not only does this method encourage interaction with users in their own environment, it also situates the librarian as a member of their community. This redefined identity enables the librarian to be more approachable, better able to anticipate patron needs, and better able to inform users of appropriate services much earlier than before. The following examples illustrate this emerging outreach tactic:

• Social networking Web sites, such as *MySpace* and *Facebook*, enable members to upload photos, link to videos, and send messages. Libraries have attempted to enter this social sphere by developing profiles and "group" spaces to promote events and deliver news and updates about their services. A more interactive strategy is to join course groups and offer targeted assistance based on actual assignments. For example, a mechanical engineering design class requires students to develop a product. This assignment involves a multitude of resources, including engineering safety standards and specifications, patents, materials data, labor cost estimates, business plan guides, and industry information. A librarian can anticipate these information needs and use *Facebook* applications to send directed messages to these particular students. Instead of relying on just the traditional one hour library instruction session, librarians have immediate access to students and can work incrementally to help them throughout the semester.

• Course management systems, including *Blackboard* and *Sakai*, provide opportunities for librarians to become *embedded* within a class. Students rely on these Web sites to interact with their professors or teaching assistants, and to access grades, the syllabus, and assignment information. Librarians can send messages to students, post instructional content, and contribute on message boards. This environment enables active participation through the ability to follow class discussions and to offer insight when it is appropriate.

• RSS aggregators, such as *Bloglines* and *Google Reader*, are helpful at pulling together an assortment of blogs, news feeds, and other syndicated information. Librarians can create personalized accounts for faculty and researchers that include table of contents updates, keyword alerts, grant and funding opportunities, and additional data. These services allow librarians to assist faculty with customized current awareness searches and to promote the value of resources (Stephens 2006).

• Collaboration with media outlets also provides mutual benefits. The Johnson County Library in Shawnee Mission, Kansas, partners with *The Kansas City Star* to offer information that is useful to readers. The business reference team prepares weekly information packages that are placed on the newspaper's Web site and link back to the library. The librarians strive "to provide information before it is needed and even before users think of the question" (*Library Journal* 2007).

These examples demonstrate how to apply technology to interact with our users in a more progressive manner. However, this approach is not limited to the Web, but is practiced through other forms as well: the "librarian on location" who sets up a booth or table in high traffic areas around campus and converses with those who pass by; the "roving reference" librarian who approaches patrons in the computer lab; the "librarian with a latté" who meets students in the café; and "field librarians" who are based in academic departments. All of these tactics aim to deliver reference and instruction through unexpected and more informal channels away from the desk.

The Potential of Social Networking

Social networking Web sites provide direct and immediate access to users. At the core, these sites reflect the identity of individuals, allowing them to map their social framework and to interact with acquaintances through various tools and applications. The appeal of social networking Web sites is in the freedom of expression. Members chronicle their lives, opinions, and experiences with the intent to share them with family and friends. This mutually open portal provides insight into one's personality and interests and allows for systemic updates and engagement in one's social universe.

These Web sites typically feature "groups" based upon themes of mutual interest. Most colleges and universities have a community group or blog that enables members to post questions and comments, promote events and activities, and share memories and experiences. This forum creates a dialogue among current and prospective students, as well as alumni and staff. That dialogue provides an ideal environment for librarians and academic professionals who wish to understand the perceptions of their communities. Topics range from campus policies to questions about housing, parking, and financial aid; as well as security concerns, athletics, critiques of professors, and assistance with assignments. Observation of these sites reveals the blending of social and academic activities that make up an individual's lifestyle. By harnessing the potential of these online channels, librarians can tune into patrons' needs and offer solutions. By becoming members of these communities and engaging with users, we can deliver reference and instruction via a more natural process.

Getting Started

There are so many social networking options that just getting started can be intimating. Many librarians have experimented with using the Social Web; however, there are no guidelines or clear models to adopt. Instead of trying to guess which service to use or worrying about how much time to invest, test several sites to find out what works best for you and your student population. Do not focus exclusively on one service, and do not get too attached to a particular Web site or tool, because change is constant. As users migrate to new platforms, so should you. As the Web evolves socially, it is advantageous for librarians to understand these collaborative technologies, since they will shape the creation, use, and storage of information and scholarly output.

LiveJournal, one of the easier Web sites to use when starting out, consists of a large collection of personal journals. Individual profiles are fully searchable, enabling you to identify students who are affiliated with a particular college or university. The practice of browsing entries posted by students at your institution may provide insight; however, a systematic review of your community is more beneficial. Monitoring blog entries allows you to respond to time sensitive issues and can also be used to detect reference and instruction opportunities.

The most efficient method for tracking multiple blogs or other syndicated content is using an RSS aggregator such as *Bloglines.* This utility enables you to log into one Web site which indicates when new material is available at several sites. Using the *Bloglines* service, you can generate a list of students affiliated with your campus and be notified whenever they post a new entry. While this system greatly reduces the time spent visiting each journal separately, it can generate an enormous amount of volume depending on how frequently users post. The typical student posts twice a week, but some post three or four times a day. You may wish to start with a small sample of blogs until you find a manageable workflow.

Most of the posts focus on social observations and may have little to do with library or academic related content. To maximize your time reading on-topic posts,

Bloglines offers a filtering feature that allows you to set keywords. This screening process reviews each new post for terms relevant to you such as *library, assignment, research,* and *study.* You could also add the name of your library, software titles, courses, professor names, and an array of other terms. Filtering in this way provides an organized review of a multitude of blogs, allowing you to focus on targeted opportunities to interact with students. The process enables librarians to preemptively reach students before they would typically approach a librarian for help.

The Preemptive Approach positions us to seek out patrons. Instead of creating a library blog and expecting students to subscribe, we in turn subscribe to their blogs and provide information to them when it is most relevant. Instead of creating a *MySpace* profile and expecting students to *befriend* us, we provide productivity tools they can use to interact with their peers. In addition to posting information on our Web site, we can place it on virtual message boards where it fits into a social context. The library becomes ubiquitous by using multiple channels, and therefore, more visible and relevant to patrons.

With a greater emphasis on social interaction, the matter of privacy is of some concern. Even though they can control accessibility and limit viewers, students may be apprehensive about welcoming authority figures, such as parents, professors and librarians, into their private Web space. However, by keeping interactions focused on course work, assignments, and academia, a librarian presence is not necessarily off-putting; students may be initially surprised, but ultimately are grateful for assistance.

Reading Library Related Postings

Perhaps the greatest value of reading student blogs is access to uncensored patron perspectives. Many posts result in a threaded discussion among friends that provides deeper insight. The follow examples illustrate the types of topics you might find:

- Confusion over library policies and practices
- Disagreement or disgruntlement over fines and recalls
- Poor customer service experiences
- Frustration using library Web sites or databases
- Students seeking research help from peers
- Discussion on course lectures and assignments
- General criticism in areas such as noise, limited study space, collections, and operating hours

Blog postings can provide us with a glance of how the library is seen through student eyes. There is a common theme of frustration and misunderstanding that emerges. By better understanding students and how they view the library, we can promote services and resources more effectively. As an assessment tool, student blogs are unparalleled because users chronicle their thoughts, providing us with unobtrusive access to their needs, experiences, and opinions. Conversely, formal assessment efforts, such as focus groups and surveys, can be limiting because participants want to give an acceptable answer (or simply ask for more of what is currently provided) rather than breaking their preconceived ideas and imagining other possibilities. Whether or not librarians choose to interact with patrons in this format, it is beneficial to at least monitor these sites for a richer understanding of the patron community and to more fully comprehend how library services are perceived and used.

Tips for Interacting with Students Online
  • *Be yourself.* A generic "library" account does not receive the same level of consideration as an individual's account. Students prefer real people over a faceless entity that is part of the institution. Create a unique profile that fosters a personal connection. Be authentic by using the tools personally and professionally, because students will respond better if you appear more believable. Be friendly, supportive, and respectful—but do not try to be their best friend.
  • *Comment only when appropriate.* When you first enter into social networking, the volume of activity can be overwhelming. While outsiders may be welcomed as observers, their opinions are not always sought. Stick to commenting on research and academic related topics, and know when to remain silent.
  • *Do not spam.* Many students use these forums to promote events, clubs, and activities around campus. While it is suitable to describe library resources and services on your own account, do not plaster community and individuals' blogs with database information or library workshop schedules, unless it is relevant to a topic. Violators of site anti-spam policies may be blocked—so familiarize yourself with the rules and guidelines for each site.
  • *Talk with library staff.* Share comments and observations regularly with colleagues. Treat these findings as you would a focus group or survey. Understanding the patron's perspective can better inform organizational decision-making and improve library experiences for everyone.
  • *Do not take it personally.* Keep in mind that you are entering their space. We should not pass judgment on our students. Be prepared for complaints about the library, professors, and the school in general. Librarians should not enter this environment as missionaries, but rather as participants; it is not our role to criticize students, but to gather their opinions and provide assistance when possible.
  • *Have fun.* Do not be too stuffy or formal. Embrace the creative freedom of expression and seek to contribute to this environment rather than control it.

Future Trends and Conclusion

In August of 2005 there were only a handful of librarians on *Facebook* and fewer than ten library outreach groups designed for interacting with students. In August of 2006, when *Facebook* eliminated department accounts, there were nearly one hundred library profiles in the *Facebook* group *Librarians and Facebook*. In December of 2007 membership in that group has reached almost four thousand. This rapid growth illustrates the shifting practice of librarians entering online social spaces populated by students. This practice will most likely increase as more librarians seek to reach students beyond the desk and outside of the classroom. A recent trend has been the inclusion of subject guides, instructional screencasts, video tours, and federated search tools designed for various Web 2.0 platforms. While librarians will undoubtedly expand their presence on the social Web, will they adopt a more proactive approach or simply provide content and utilities for students to discover on their own? In many ways, librarians are simply recreating their library Web sites, rather than providing a new and interactive experience. Consideration must also be given to the longevity of these Web sites; although they are popular with college students, will they retain their mainstream appeal? It is important that librarians not get too comfortable using one Web site, but rather, continuously explore new Web 2.0 tools as they emerge.

Social networking Web sites provide an immense opportunity for library outreach. Never before have we had this level of access to our users. These tools not only enable us to promote and deliver services and resources in a targeted format, but also to measure library usage and effectiveness and to gather genuine impressions from our patron communities. While reference desk transactions may be declining, students still have complex information needs and often turn to peers for help. This trend is evidenced through blogs and social networking sites, where students rely on friends for assistance. By harnessing these technologies and tapping into specialized online communities, librarians can reach patrons who might not have considered using the library otherwise. It is imperative that we expand this philosophical shift in our approach to public services and seek to make libraries more immersive. As information usage increasingly becomes a Web-based social process, librarians need to be in on the conversation. By adopting a preemptive attitude and constantly seeking opportunities to engage users, the library becomes a genuine partner in the learning process, rather than filling a supporting role.

Sources for Additional Research

Farkas, M. G. 2007. *Social software in libraries: Building collaboration, communication, and community online.* Medford, NJ: Information Today.
This book examines the growth of social software and how these technologies can be applied in libraries.

Jessi H. and P. Lehman. 2005. The MySpace generation. *Business Week* Issue 3963: 86-96.
This article provides an overview on the impact of the Web on teens, and how they use blogs and online social networking to communicate.

Mathews, B. S. 2006. Do you Facebook? Networking with students online. *College & Research Libraries News* 67 (5): 306-8.
This article provides an early look at using *Facebook* to provide preemptive reference.

Mathews, B.S. *The Ubiquitous Librarian.* http://theubiquitouslibrarian.typepad.com
This is the author's blog chronicling experiments in outreach and the social Web.

McKiernan, G. *Friends: Social Networking Sites for Engaged Library Services.*
http://onlinesocialnetworks.blogspot.com/.
This blog is devoted to the use of online social networking Web sites for any and all
types of library-related programs or services.

Works Cited

Atlas, M. C., D. P. Wallace, and C. V. Fleet. 2005. Library anxiety in the electronic era,
or why won't anybody talk to me anymore? *Reference & User Services Quarterly* 44
(4): 314-19.

De Rosa, C. and others, eds. 2005. *Perceptions of libraries and information resources.* Dublin,
OH: OCLC Online Computer Library Center, Inc. http://www.loc.gov/catdir/toc/
fy0708/2006367596.html.

Library Journal. 2007. Library presents "preemptive reference". *Library Journal* 132 (6):
13.

Kyrillidou, M. 2000. Research library trends: ARL statistics. *Journal of Academic Librarianship* 26 (6): 427-36.

Onwuegbuzie, A.J., Q.G. Jiao, and S.L. Bostick. 2004. *Library anxiety: Theory, research,
and applications.* New York: Scarecrow Press.

Stephens, M. 2006. Selling RSS to medical librarians. *Tame the Web: Libraries and
Technology Blog,* [June 2006], http://tametheweb.com/2006/06/ttw_mailbox_sell-
ing_rss_to_med.html.

Thomsett-Scott, B., and P.E. Reese. 2006. Changes in library technology and reference desk
statistics: Is there a relationship? *Public Services Quarterly* 2 (2/3): 143-165.

CHAPTER 9

Wikis and Collaborative Reference Services

John Russell

Librarians have long been concerned with connecting researchers with information, typically (but by no means exclusively) through face-to-face contact at a reference desk. With the advent of the Internet and the proliferation of online resources and services, librarians have used Web-based resources to add an asynchronous dimension to traditional synchronic reference services. One of the new Web-based technologies that has been discussed by librarians in the past few years is the wiki. Librarians have been using wikis for a variety of purposes, including research guides, knowledge-bases, and library Web sites (see Farkas 2005, Chawner and Lewis 2006, and Wikis 2007 for a number of examples), though they are flexible enough to work in most situations where collaboration or quick Web editing are desired. Wikis are an attractive tool for reference services because they are a relatively simple and inexpensive way to improve information flows among librarians and between librarians and their campus community.

What are Wikis?

Put very simply, wikis are Web pages that allow readers to edit the pages directly in their Web browsers. Typically, someone who wants to edit a Web page must download a file from a server, modify its code, and then upload the file to the server. Someone who wants to edit a wiki, on the other hand, can enter new information on the Web page simply by clicking "Edit." Wikis are also different from standard Web pages in that they use a simplified markup language that is not based on HTML. For example, a link to an external Web page in a wiki can be created simply by typing in the full URL, whereas an HTML-based Web page requires the use of <a> tags. Less concretely, wikis are also notable for the culture of open-authorship that they create; in fact, the "author" of a wiki, especially one with an active community of participants who regularly refine content, can be difficult to identify. The last important aspect of wikis is that they are living documents, since at any time a reader can update content (see Lamb 2004 or Chawner and Lewis 2006 for more on wiki typology and use). It is important to note that openness to anyone and everyone is not an essential characteristic of wikis: there are wikis that are password-protected so that only a select few can edit (or in some cases, read) the wiki.

Wikis and Academic Libraries

Librarians have already begun to explore the ways that wikis can enhance connections between libraries and the communities that they serve. Wikis have been used as content management systems (Chawner and Lewis 2006), to help with instruction (Allan 2007 and Deitering and Bridgewater 2007), and for general professional development (Wikis 2007). The examples below, which touch on both current and potential uses, focus on how wikis can be used for reference services.

Subject Guides

The Web-based subject guide is a common part of any academic library's Web presence. Librarians create these guides to enable researchers to identify and access subject specific databases or other reference resources. These subject guides can also be useful for librarians at the reference desk, both as guides for the researcher and as aides to the librarian who may be unfamiliar with the subject area and the specialized resources associated with it. Because of the importance of subject guides to reference librarians, most discussion of wikis in academic libraries involves at least a mention of their utility in creating these guides. The most well-known example of a wiki subject guide is the *Biz Wiki* at Ohio University (Boeninger 2007).

Biz Wiki was created by Chad Boeninger to make updating his subject guides more manageable. Boeninger was dissatisfied with his pre-existing research guides due to the redundancy of resources across the guides, the lack of interlinking between guides, the extra work involved in updating or editing content in multiple places, and the lack of searchability (Boeninger 2005). Boeninger's use of a wiki allowed him to create a more flexible and responsive research guide; with the "popular pages" feature of his wiki he was also able to measure use of the guide more accurately. Another important aspect of the wiki that Boeninger extols is the ability to add content "on the fly." He explains how he was able to take an answer from an e-mail reference question and add it to the wiki while he was answering a similar question via instant messaging; Boeninger was thus able to point the person on IM to this newly created page (Boeninger 2005). Although other librarians, such as those at Florida State University, are starting to adopt wikis as a platform for subject guides, the practice is not yet widespread (Jackson and Blackburn 2007).

An adjunct to the subject guides created by librarians is the course-specific guide, which can be both an aid to instruction and a more targeted resource for faculty and students. In 2006, I tried an experiment with a history course where I set up a wiki (http://gsuhist3000.pbwiki.com/) for use as a more open, flexible course guide (though one that was password protected so that only the class could edit it). The object was to create a space where the students and professor could recommend resources to each other, but in such a way that I was also privy to these recommendations and thus could amend them (in case erroneous information was offered) or add suggestions. Nine students (out of a class of thirty) and the professor added content; much of the rest was a modified version of a librarian-created course guide (often modified in response to student comments). Discussions with a few of the students and with the professor suggested that unfamiliarity with using wikis and the absence of a participation requirement were major factors in the low percentage of users; the lack of a sense of community may also have played a role (see Deitering and Bridgewater 2007 and Walker 2006 for good discussions about the importance of community in wiki success). Despite the mixed results, the underlying premise is still valid: wikis provide a platform for an interactive conversation among students, faculty, and librarians. More significantly, introducing a wiki into a course reinforces the importance of the social aspects of information literacy. By making collaboration a focus, students experience how information sharing is central to a community of scholars.

Reference Manuals

Reference manuals are also a common part of the reference librarian's experience. These manuals are important for establishing policies and can be crucial for training, but, when they are paper-based, keeping them current can be time-consuming. Wikis are a natural fit for reference manuals because they are searchable and are designed for quick editing. The Australian Catholic University Library has used a wiki-based reference manual as an antidote to inadequate indexing and problems with currency (Blake 2006, 4) and librarians at Georgia State University created an Intranet wiki that provides a central point for accessing the reference manual and other library policies, guides, and even price quotes from vendors (Glogowski and Steiner 2008, forthcoming).

Campus Knowledge-Base

Most librarians are accustomed to receiving non-library related questions at the reference desk. These kinds of questions present a great opportunity for providing seamless service at the campus level, but they can sometimes be quite difficult to answer quickly. A librarian could set up a wiki to act as a knowledge-base rather than taking on the more onerous task of database development and management. Ideally, other campus departments could participate directly by having the ability to edit the wiki: this level of access would ensure that the wiki's content was current and reliable and would also increase the visibility of the resource. Such a campus-oriented wiki could also be used for training residence advisors or other peer assistants who need a reliable source of information about a variety of campus services. Of course, the success of the wiki would depend on getting acceptance from a variety of sources but, if successful, the wiki could symbolize the library's place at the hub of campus information flows.

Readers' Advisory

Another possibility for wiki implementation is the creation of a reader's advisory wiki. The *Butler WikiRef* (http://www.seedwiki.com/wiki/butler_wikiref/) is an attempt at this, as the wiki is set up to be an annotated guide to reference sources available via the Butler University Libraries. What I envision is broader: a resource where librarians, students, and faculty can recommend books to each other. Looking for a good mystery novel, monologues for an audition, or the best book to read for an introduction to Shakespeare? The reader's advisory wiki would be the place for all of that and be both browseable by topic and fully searchable. In its broadest implementation, such a wiki could supplant subject and course guides by becoming a master guide to a variety of topics. Even with a narrow implementation, such as an annotated list of important material on a specific topic (e.g., World War I or graphic novels) or collaboration with various librarians on a more interdisciplinary topic, a reader's advisory wiki makes tacit knowledge explicit by getting more experienced advice out on the Internet where it is more accessible.

What Kinds of Problems Can Be Expected?

While proponents often note how easy wikis are to use, there is still a learning curve. Most people who have never seen a wiki before are not going to be able to sit down and make one work immediately; in fact, telling new users how easy wikis are can discourage those who initially struggle (Walker 2006, 69-70). Furthermore, knowing how to edit a wiki does not mean that one knows how to make use of one or that an individual is automatically comfortable with the idea of editing "someone else's work" (Walker 2006, 73; Deitering and Bridgewater 2007, 40; Wiebrands 2006). Make time for training and do not underestimate the amount of training required. Consider adding detailed help pages or supply cheat sheets that users can download and look at while editing the wiki. Depending on the context, it might also be useful to have a link to an "Ask-a-Librarian" page or to embed a chat widget in order to provide another layer of assistance to users.

Although wikis are living documents that are open to editing by multiple authors, they should not be created and then ignored. At least one person should tend the wiki to ensure appropriate use and make corrections as the need arises (Wiebrands 2006). Spam can also be a problem for wikis that are open to editing by anyone, so in these instances one needs either a very active community of users who take responsibility for deleting spam or an installation of anti-spam software (Chawner and Lewis 2006, 39; Farkas 2005). If the organizational structure of the wiki is left open, sometimes the result can be a resource where specific information is difficult to find. In situations where setting standards or guidelines might be helpful (e.g., for ensuring usability or eliminating uncertainty as a way of encouraging content), have someone in charge of the wiki who can create a structure for contributions (Chawner and Lewis 2006, 43; Deitering and Bridgewater 2007, 32-33; Glogowski and Steiner 2008, forthcoming).

Many people fall prey to the idea that technology has inherent qualities that transfer immediately to the environment into which the technology has been introduced. Wikis, like any technology, are tools and thus are extensions of human practice: they need an active community in order to flourish. Having a wiki attached to one's library Web site will not magically attract people who will fall under its spell and feverishly use it. As Deitering and Bridgewater (2007) show so well, a successful wiki requires work: it has to be marketed, tended to, and sometimes reconceptualized based on user feedback. If there are not sufficient resources (in terms of staff time or community interest) to keep the wiki vibrant and well-groomed, then it might be best not to start one at all. Nothing is more dispiriting than putting effort into starting a new project only to have it flounder. Before undertaking a wiki project, be sure to plan in advance and take into consideration who the stakeholders are and how to ensure their continued interest.

Conclusion

If you can think of a time in your professional life when you were frustrated with keeping the phone numbers and URLs in your reference manual up to date, when you wished that you did not have to call someone in Systems to make a simple edit to your library's Web page, or when you wanted to collaborate more with students or faculty, then wikis might be the right tool for you. Many librarians might be daunted by the thought of inviting others to participate in reference services, but opportunities for collaboration with students, faculty, and campus staff are a way of tapping into the expertise of our community. If the ultimate goal is to connect researchers with the best information available, then librarians need to harness the knowledge and experience that exists on any academic campus. Wikis provide the means for individuals to share their expertise, provide a way to reduce barriers to information, and thus are a way to improve the quality of reference services.

Sources for Additional Research

Chawner, B. and P. H. Lewis. 2006. WikiWikiWebs: New ways to communicate in a Web environment. *Information Technology and Libraries* 25 (1): 33-43.
> This article presents a thorough introduction to wiki history, technology, and uses, with in-depth explanations of wiki concepts and implementation. The authors note a couple disadvantages of wikis (spam, lack of markup standardization) and enumerate factors for a successful wiki.

Deitering, A. and R. Bridgewater. 2005. Stop reinventing the wheel: Using wikis for professional knowledge sharing. *Journal of Web Librarianship* 1 (1): 27-44.
> This article details the creation of the *Library Instruction Wiki* (http://instructionwiki. org) in great depth. The authors highlight the need for marketing, encouraging a sense of community ownership, responsiveness to feedback from users, and extensive preparatory work to make a wiki successful.

Farkas, M. 2005. So you want to build a wiki? *WebJunction* (September 1, 2005), http:// webjunction.org/do/DisplayContent?id=11262.
> This article provides a sensible overview of the planning process, common problems, and an introduction to the most popular wiki software.

Kille, A. 2006. Wikis in the workplace: How wikis can help manage knowledge in library reference services. *LIBRES* 16 (1). http://libres.curtin.edu.au/libres16n1/Kille_essayo-pinion.htm.
> Kille's article provides a thorough discussion of wikis and the role that they can play in knowledge management. It provides a good point of entry into the knowledge management literature.

Lamb, B. 2004. Wide open spaces: Wikis, ready or not. *EDUCAUSE Review* 39 (5): 36-48.
This article is heavily cited, in part because it was one of the first articles to address the current and potential uses of wikis in higher education. It covers the history of wikis and surveys the technical aspects with the non-expert user in mind.

Walker, J. P., Jr. 2006. Identifying and overcoming barriers to the successful adoption and use of wikis in collaborative knowledge management. Honor's thesis, University of North Carolina at Chapel Hill. http://hdl.handle.net/1901/267.
Based on qualitative and quantitative analysis of wiki use by Information & Library Science students at the University of North Carolina at Chapel Hill, Walker's research provides a welcome empirical basis for further discussion regarding the barriers that can impede the success of a wiki: the absence of a strong community; lack of technical proficiency; and perceptions of lack of knowledge/expertise.

Wikis. 2007. *Library success: A best practices wiki.* http://www.libsuccess.org/index. php?title=Wikis.
This wiki provides a useful list of links to library-related wikis and also has a short list of suggested readings. Be sure to add your library to it when you try some of the ideas presented in this chapter!

Works Cited

Allan, C. 2007. Using a wiki to manage a library instruction program: Sharing knowledge to better serve patrons. *College & Research Library News* 68 (4). http://www.ala.org/ala/acrl/acrlpubs/crlnews/backissues2007/april07/usingawiki.htm.

Blake, P. 2006. Using a wiki for information services: Principles and practicalities. Presented at the Australian Library and Information Association New Librarians' Symposium 2006, December 1-2, 2006, Sydney, Australia. http://www.information-online.com.au/docs/Presentations/ using_a_wiki_for_information_services_(io2007_paper).pdf.

Boeninger, C. 2005. Wikis in action: A wiki as a research guide. Presented at Computers in Libraries, March 22, 2006, Washington, DC http://www.infotoday.com/cil2006/presentations/C101-102_Boeninger.pps.

Boeninger, C. 2007. Biz Wiki. http://www.library.ohiou.edu/subjects/bizwiki/index.php/Main_Page.

Chawner, B. and P. H. Lewis. 2006. WikiWikiWebs: New ways to communicate in a Web environment. *Information Technology and Libraries* 25 (1): 33-43.

Deitering, A. and R. Bridgewater. 2005. Stop reinventing the wheel: Using wikis for professional knowledge sharing. *Journal of Web Librarianship* 1 (1): 27-44.

Farkas, M. 2005. So you want to build a wiki? *WebJunction* (September 1, 2005), http://webjunction.org/do/DisplayContent?id=11262.

Jackson, M. and J. Blackburn. 2007. MediaWiki open source software as infrastructure for electronic resource outreach. Presented at Electronic Resources & Libraries Conference, February 24, 2007, Atlanta, GA. http://hdl.handle.net/1853/13647.

Lamb, B. 2004. Wide open spaces: Wikis, ready or not. *EDUCAUSE Review* 39 (5): 36-48.

Online reference. 2007. *Library Success: A Best Practices Wiki.* http://www.libsuccess.org/index.php?title=Online_Reference.

Glogowski, J. and S. Steiner. 2008. The life of a wiki: How Georgia State University Library's wiki enhances content currency and employee collaboration. *Internet Reference Services Quarterly* 13 (1) (forthcoming). http://hdl.handle.net/2197/269.

Walker, J. P., Jr. 2006. Identifying and overcoming barriers to the successful adoption and use of wikis in collaborative knowledge management. Honor's thesis, University of North Carolina at Chapel Hill. http://hdl.handle.net/1901/267.

Wiebrands, C. 2006. Collaboration and communication via wiki: The experience of Curtin University Library and Information Service. Presented at the Australian Library and Information Association 2006 Biennial Conference, Perth, Australia, September 19-22. http://conferences.alia.org.au/alia2006/Papers/Constance_Wiebrands_2.pdf.

Wikis. 2007. *Library success: A best practices wiki.* http://www.libsuccess.org/index.php?title=Wikis.

CHAPTER 10

Get in the Game: Adapting Library Services to the Needs of Gamers

Chad F. Boeninger

Libraries—and librarians—change constantly to meet their users' needs. During their careers, many veteran librarians have witnessed the transition from card catalogs to Online Public Access Catalogs, have facilitated the shift from print indexes to computer indexes on floppy disk or CD-ROMs, and have welcomed online searching and indexing via the Internet. Libraries and librarians have always been able to adapt to technological change, and in many ways have been leaders in this area. Their ability to change with the times and meet the technology and information needs of patrons has enabled libraries to remain relevant, despite many fears that the Internet would put them out of business.

With the experience of technological change, librarians are now looking at new ways to enhance the end-user experience. Many individuals in libraries and information organizations are attempting to understand patron needs, information-seeking behavior, and user demographics through focus groups, surveys, and even extensive research studies. It is important to study specific demographic groups, whether they be Gen Xers, Millennials, or Boomers; the study of these groups offers information that can help a library decide which collections to buy, how to construct new facilities, which services to offer, and how to teach patrons. Librarians can learn a great deal about patrons by recording how they interact with Web interfaces, observing how and where they study, being aware of their leisure activities, and understanding what types of media they purchase or use.

Increasingly, patrons are purchasing and using video games. Video gaming is one leisure activity that deserves more attention from libraries and librarians. The video game industry brings in seven billion dollars a year, and its success depends on producing products that are entertaining and engaging (Electronic Software Association 2007). These games are often quite lengthy, complex, and at times, frustrating; they require players to spend large amounts of time exploring, learning, and mastering the games. By studying how video games attract players, retain their attention, and make them learn, librarians can incorporate many gaming principles into existing library services, resources, and instruction, and can enhance the library experience for their patrons.

Really? "Study" Video Games?

Librarians may wonder why we would want to study video games when there are so many other technologies and media for us to attempt to master. The study of video games is a relatively new discipline, but it is beginning to gain prominence in academic circles. Authors such as James Gee and Mark Prensky have written extensively on the topic, and they contend that video games have an important impact on those who play them. They also assert that by studying video games, educators, policy makers, and others can adapt game characteristics for the educational curriculum (Prensky 2006, 254; Gee 2004, 225). As librarians, we can learn from Gee and Prensky (and from video games as well) in order to get a better idea about our users' backgrounds and preferences.

A primary job of the reference librarian is to help patrons find information about a particular topic in order to satisfy an information need. In helping them with this need, librarians teach patrons research and critical thinking skills while helping them learn to adapt to a constantly changing information environment. Librarians understand that research can be a very difficult process that often results in high levels of anxiety, frustration, confusion, and even anger. Though many people consider them to be mindless entertainment, video games can be very complex and take a great deal of time and mastery to complete. As Steven Johnson explains:

> The first and last thing that should be said about the experience of play-ing today's video games, the thing that you almost never hear about in the mainstream coverage, is that games are fiendishly, sometimes mad-deningly, *hard*. The dirty little secret of gaming is how much time you spend not having fun. You may be confused, you may be disoriented, you may be stuck. When you put the game down and move back into the real world you may find yourself mentally working through the problem you've been wrestling with, as though you are worrying a loose tooth. If this is mindless escapism, it's a strangely masochistic version. Who wants to escape to a world that irritates you 90% of the time? (Johnson 2006, 25-26)

Johnson's description of the difficulty of video games draws upon some similar characteristics of information seeking behavior. Both video game quests and research quests can be hard and frustrating and may lead to disorientation, confusion, and anger. However, gamers welcome the challenge of a difficult video game and often do their best to master a game. By studying the attraction of video games, librarians may understand this motivation and get patrons motivated in the same way about library research.

One of the difficulties that librarians face is the communication barrier be-tween themselves and their patrons. When helping patrons at the reference desk, on the phone, or via instant message or chat, librarians generally provide better service when they avoid use of library jargon. However, it is not always easy to determine the most effective way to communicate with a particular patron, since professors, college students, retirees, international students, Millennials, and even gamers have different needs. Gamers may see things differently, as explained by John Beck and Mitchell Wade:

> This generation is literally growing up in the world of videogames. That world is completely different from the one all of us grew up in. And grow-

ing up there is making this generation—our kids—visibly, measurably different. They can handle reality all right—in some ways better than we do. All those hours spent playing video games are teaching them important skills. But they don't see things the way nongamers do and they don't maneuver the same way. For their great new skills to work in our nongamer world, they need some help adapting. (Beck and Wade 2006, xii)

With a better understanding of gamers, librarians can help them adapt to the information environment while adapting to gamers' information needs.

Many people assume that gamers are a small minority of the population that consists primarily of adolescent boys. If this assumption were true, it might not be worthwhile to spend time attempting to understand them. However, according to the Electronic Software Association, gaming is a great deal more prevalent than one would think. According to the Association's 2007 *Essential Facts about the Computer and Video Game Industry*, 28.2 percent of gamers are under eighteen years of age, 47.6 percent are eighteen to forty-nine years of age, and 24.2 percent are over the age of fifty. In addition, the average age of the game player is thirty-three years old, and sixty-nine percent of American heads of households play computer or video games. While game playing is still a very male dominated activity, female gamers make up thirty-eight percent of the gaming population. At the same time, women eighteen years or older represent thirty percent of the overall gaming population, ahead of the twenty percent occupied by boys younger than seventeen (Electronic Software Association 2007). Furthermore, the gaming population is likely to grow; consultant firm PricewaterhouseCoopers has projected that the sales for computer and video games will be larger than music sales in the United States in 2009. In the U.S alone, sales of video games are projected to grow to over twelve billion dollars by 2011 (Graft 2007).

Scholars have recognized the impact that video games have on popular culture and the economy while also studying the impact of games on education and learning. Prensky (*Don't Bother Me Mom, I'm Learning*), Gee (*What Video Games Have to Teach Us About Literacy and Learning*), and Johnson (*Everything Bad is Good For You*) all offer their opinions and observations about what makes gaming so compelling to consumers. Each book is highly recommended for more in-depth discussion of video games and learning that goes beyond the scope of this chapter. From these discussions about gaming and learning, one can see that there are common traits that libraries share with video games. In a sense, both video games and libraries attempt to immerse the player or patron, encourage learning by doing, and encourage exploration.

An Immersive Environment

When selecting a video game, gamers may look at different sources and base their purchasing decisions on multiple criteria. There are multiple Web sites, blogs, and magazines that help consumers with purchasing decisions through reviews. Most reviews are based upon the elements of gameplay, sound, graphics, presentation, and replay value, and the best games receive high marks in almost all categories. Each of these criteria helps to draw the player into the game.

Most highly-rated games—particularly action, adventure, and role playing ones—contain a story that immerses and engages the player. A player may initially select a game based upon the character that he gets to play, or because he is drawn to the story, but he is more likely to continue playing if the story is interesting throughout the game. Part of playing a video game is not only beating up the bad guys or shooting the enemy, but also being rewarded with successful progression of the game with new plot twists in the storyline. The drive to see what happens next immerses the player in the game environment and motivates him to keep playing. At the same time, a game whose story turns sour at the half-way point may cause a player to quit playing.

Sony's *God of War*, hailed as one of the best PlayStation 2 games of all time, is an example of a game with an incredibly immersive story. The game begins with the game's antagonist, Kratos, jumping off a cliff. The player does not know why Kratos is choosing to end his life, nor does he know the details or events that lead him to his decision. Before Kratos crashes into the rocks at the bottom of the cliff, the game takes the player to a time three weeks earlier and places the player in control of Kratos. The game takes the player about fifteen hours to complete, and along the way he will learn more about the character Kratos. The player only knows a little bit of the story at the beginning, but the more the player progresses through the game, the more he learns.

Games also use customization features to immerse the player. Many games allow the player to customize a variety of elements in order to make the game more engrossing. Role playing games, or RPGs, offer perhaps the greatest amount of customization. As players progress, they get skill points that can be assigned to various characters that they control. This process, called "leveling up," allows a player to assign points to skill areas that are determined by his playing style. If the player is more likely to use magic in a battle than his character's sword, then he will likely assign more points to the character's magical abilities.

Examples of leveling up can be found in a number of different games. *Resident Evil 4* (RE4), another highly-acclaimed PlayStation 2 and Nintendo Gamecube game, uses this leveling up system to allow a player to take control of his own game. In RE4, the player controls Leon as he works his way through a Spanish town in order to find the President's daughter. During his quest to find her, Leon is confronted by thousands of angry villagers and multiple monsters that are determined to stop and kill him. As Leon defeats his foes, he is rewarded with money, ammunition, health packs, medicinal herbs, and more. Unfortunately, Leon's attaché bag will only hold so much, so the player must decide which objects he will keep as Leon accrues more items. If the player values ammunition over life-sustaining items, he will likely discard the medicinal herbs for the shotgun shells. Such a decision can have a large impact on the gameplay, as the player may reach a point in the game where it would serve Leon better to have more health and less firepower.

RE4 also forces the player to make decisions with limited resources. As Leon accumulates money, the player can buy new weapons for him or upgrade existing ones. As with collecting ammunition and medicinal herbs, the player may also have to sell one of Leon's weapons to make room in his attaché bag for a new one. Doing so can be risky, as the player does not know if ammunition for the machine gun that he just purchased will be as plentiful as the bullets for the pistol that he just sold. In a sense, this risk taking and decision making puts players in control of their own destinies by allowing an increased feeling of immersion in the game. While in its simplest form RE4 is about shooting things and solving puzzles, the character customization elements add a great deal of complexity, thereby drawing the player further into the game.

So how do libraries create immersive environments for library patrons? Our shelves are full of good stories, but are books enough to engage users and bring them back for more? After all, many of our users are turning to Barnes & Noble when they would like to browse for books in a comfortable environment. Librarians all over the world are investigating ways to address this question, and there is no one answer for every single library. There are, however, a number of tactics that librarians can try in order to make their environments more engaging for their users.

While it may be difficult for librarians to create epic stories on the scale of *God of War*, they can do many things to make sure that they offer compelling content that is useful to the communities that they serve. By soliciting input from the user community, libraries can offer relevant and engaging content that will appeal to library users. Community-building exercises, such as book clubs and other social interactions, can help to immerse patrons in the library environment and enable them to direct their own library experience.

Gamers are used to customizing their environments, and Web 2.0 tools can give libraries the ability to create personalized options for users which may rival in-game experiences. Many tools allow for user-created content, tagging, and participation, and enable patrons to have shared experiences with other library users. Other options for personalization include library portals that allow users to create personal library home pages. Applications such as *MyLibrary* enable users to create links to their favorite library resources and customize their virtual library experiences.

Library tutorials can also be immersive environments. Tools such as *Captivate* and *Camtasia* empower librarians to easily make *Flash*-based demonstrations, screencasts, and tutorials. One way to engage users with these types of tutorials is to create sessions that incorporate decision trees. A decision tree is an element that many games use to allow the player to control his path through the game. Decision making can be introduced into library research tutorials in order to make the tutorial more engaging for the user. Rather than simply watching a demonstration of a database or research skill, the user might be able to control where the tutorial goes by making a particular decision. This interactivity gives the user a small amount of ownership in the tutorial, as the decisions that he makes directly impact the personal experience. As an example, a library tutorial can allow users to choose what they believe to be the most-reliable resource for a given topic, and then show them the implications of their choice of resource. While tutorials that incorporate decision trees will be more complicated to design and build, the end product will result in a product that is more heavily used by the library community.

Learning by Doing

Video games not only immerse the player in the game environment, but they also deliver complex instructions along the way. Highly-rated video games often earn their ranking because they are intuitive and engaging. Video games are usually packaged with user manuals which highlight the basic controls of the video game. However, simply reading the manual can prove very difficult because, as Gee comments (Gee 2004, 101-103), learning the manual is not in the context of playing the game. As such, most successful games offer a pick-up-and-play simplicity in the beginning which encourages the player to learn through participation. Librarians can learn a great deal from the active learning mechanisms that video games employ.

To illustrate how games allow the player to learn by doing, it helps to look at an actual game scenario. *God of War*, discussed previously, has one of the most intuitive control mechanisms available. While the game uses all sixteen buttons on the PlayStation 2 controller, it introduces those buttons (and their various combinations) over a period of time. The instruction manual that comes with the game does have a diagram of the controller with descriptions of each action assigned to the sixteen buttons, but the illustration is primarily intended as a quick reference guide. The diagram is not intended to be the primary instruction mechanism, as the buttons and descriptions can be intimidating to the beginning player. If the manual were the only way for the player to learn the game, he would have to spend more time studying the manual in order to play. Many experienced gamers would tire of this quickly, and perhaps would go find another, more intuitive game to play. Game developers recognize this tendency and therefore use the game itself to teach the player the necessary controls and actions.

After Kratos jumps from the cliff and before he crashes into the rocks below, the story travels back in time to three weeks earlier. The player is launched immediately into the action of the game and finds himself controlling Kratos on a boat in the middle of a raging storm in the Aegean Sea. Suddenly, snarling creatures rush at Kratos with swords and spears, and Kratos must fight them off. The player must immediately learn how to use some of the game's controls in order to fend off the creatures. In reaction, avid gamers start mashing buttons on the controller to see what Kratos will do, and after a minute, the player is presented with on-screen dialogue that directs him to press the square button for a light attack and the triangle button for a heavy attack. The player also learns to press the circle button to grab enemies, and to press the R2 button to open treasure chests and doors. All of these instructions are issued to the player while he is playing the game, so that he can immediately practice and apply the new skill. The player is even instructed on how to block enemy blows by pressing the R1 button, a skill that is learned immediately before a dragon crashes through the hull of Kratos' ship and attacks him. In fact, during the first few minutes of the game, the player builds an arsenal of skills: he can deploy light and heavy attacks, grab enemies, block enemies, launch enemies, open objects, balance on small beams, move and push objects, evade attacks, and save the game—actions which require using eight of the sixteen buttons on the controller.

If learning these skills was all there was to playing and beating the game, players might quickly grow tired of the experience. Players would easily master the various buttons and would probably get bored in a short period of time. However, games like *God of War* gradually increase in difficulty as the player progresses, requiring the player to acquire and master new skills each time he confronts new challenges and enemies. This gradual instruction method is often difficult for developers to get right, so some games begin very easy and then grow more difficult, while others are very difficult from the beginning. There is a fine balance between teaching players and boring them with instruction. *God of War* has that balance, as new skills are quickly tested by the increasing difficulty of the game.

Librarians often face the same challenges as game developers when offering instruction and reference services to library patrons. Since each patron comes to the desk or the classroom with a different research background, it is difficult for librarians to know the skill level of each patron. While most game developers know that each player begins the game at the same level, librarians do not know how much research experience each patron may have. It is therefore important for librarians to take time with each patron to assess his abilities and needs. By measuring the patron's comfort level with research, the librarian can adapt the instruction appropriately. Once the patron understands the basic skills of the research process or, for example, becomes familiar with the interface of a database, the librarian can then introduce more advanced concepts.

Many librarians recognize that learning can occur in a number of different ways and offer multiple methods of instruction. One common method is to offer a demonstration to introduce the basic skills needed to navigate a database or find articles. However, gamers prefer hands-on practice with a database to engage in active learning. Learning where to put the search terms and how to modify search fields is similar to practicing with the game controller. Without this hands-on application, the content is as irrelevant as reading a video game instruction manual without ever actually playing the game.

Unfortunately, librarians do not have the opportunity to talk to or teach every library patron, so adapting gameplay characteristics to reference and instruction services will not address every need. Librarians must also look to altering interfaces to incorporate gameplay elements. As an example, library catalogs can be intimidating to library patrons, particularly if they are accustomed to using *Google* or other search engines for research. Librarians understand the power that a library online catalog offers to library users, but they are often challenged by how to teach patrons the power of controlled vocabulary and field searching.

Many library Web sites offer a keyword search for their catalogs, and then link to advanced search options. In an effort to teach patrons about the advanced search options—for example, periodical title search, subject search, author search, and more—librarians point users to Web-based documentation about these options. Gamers, however, are not likely to read this documentation, as they are more accustomed to the system teaching them as they use it.

Perhaps librarians should strive to create catalogs and databases that are more like games. These Web-based library resources might be significantly more intuitive to users if they offered instruction while the patron was using them. For example, rather than forcing a user to read pages of documentation about the merits of controlled vocabulary and how to limit by format, a catalog could offer intuitive hints that appear during searches. If a user happened to be looking at a record for an item in the catalog, on-screen hints could highlight how to look for other items with the same subject or author. Likewise, a smarter catalog could offer suggestions on how to locate the item in the library, without requiring the user to comprehend a glossary of library terms such as "stacks," "reference", "reserves," "periodicals," or "microfilm."

Granted, many catalog and database vendors are building smarter systems, but they all offer similarly limited help options. These options require the user to navigate to the help menu and read until they find a solution to the problem. These interfaces are akin to handing a player a controller and telling him to read the manual first and then play. Gamers, and our catalog and database users, might be more inclined to use library resources if we offered options that were more intuitive with pick-up-and-play features that allowed them to learn more while using the systems.

Encouraging Exploration

While games teach players with on-screen dialogue, they do not always tell them everything that there is to know about the game. Video games give players the opportunity to figure things out for themselves through hands-on exploration. In order to advance to the next level in a game, a player may have to explore the environment and use trial and error tactics to solve a puzzle or defeat an enemy. Such exploration may require that the player repeat a particular part of a game over and over, and learning and mastery of the game is accomplished through this repetition.

One example of this exploration occurs in the game *Ico*. In *Ico*, the player assumes the role of the title character, a young boy named Ico, who must lead a young girl, Yorda, out of a treacherous castle. The game is riddled with physics-based puzzles that the player must solve in order to get the pair closer to the exit of the castle. Many of the puzzles require the player to move Ico and Yorda around a large room until he finds the best route, the right tool, or the appropriate lever to solve the puzzle. Many of the puzzles are difficult, and there is no on-screen dialogue to point the player in the right direction. Occasionally the game's camera angle will shift, offering the player a hint at his next action. One scenario occurs very early in the game, when Ico finds Yorda trapped in a cage suspended from the ceiling. The player can lead Ico around a large room to look for objects which may be used to rescue Yorda. The player may try jumping up to the cage or hitting it with a stick, but both methods prove ineffective. Scouring the room for a switch or lever yields nothing, except for a box in the corner of the room. Further exploration reveals that the box can be pushed across the room to a ledge adjacent to the cage. The player can then make Ico climb the box, shimmy up to the ledge, and then jump off of the ledge and onto the top of the suspended cage. Once Ico lands on the cage, the chain breaks, the cage falls to the ground, Yorda is freed, and the puzzle is solved.

As games encourage exploration by players, librarians can likewise encourage exploration by patrons. Rather than simply demonstrate how to find a book in a catalog, find articles in a database, or renew books online, a librarian might encourage the patron to explore the resource while she offers helpful hints. Many patrons may learn the way that gamers do, by experimenting with a Web-based interface or by trying a number of keyword possibilities. As this takes time, encouraging exploration may not be practical at a busy reference desk, but it can be used during individual reference consultation sessions. Such exploration not only benefits patrons (by allowing them to learn with hands-on use) but also helps the librarian to learn something as well. By observing the patron's exploration behaviors, the librarian can develop a better understanding of a Web site's usability, the effectiveness of library jargon, beginning searching behavior, and more.

Just as a librarian guides a patron through a research question, some games offer built-in reference resources. In *Metal Gear Solid 2: Sons of Liberty*, the player assumes the character of Snake, who must infiltrate the enemy's territory to keep them from stealing a nuclear weapon. Snake is vastly outnumbered, so the player has to move him around without being caught. The gameplay is a little more complex than other action games, as there is more to the game than simply running through the level and dispatching enemies. The game incorporates a number of different tasks, puzzles, equipment, and weapons that a player must master in order to progress. To assist with this complexity, this game offers a different sort of instructional help. As the game opens, Snake is greeted on his codec radio by Otacon, the friendly support staff member who is back at the base. As the player explores the game, Otacon (and later, the Colonel) offers advice on how to solve a problem or tells Snake what he needs to do next in the mission. For example, if the player finds a new weapon in the game, Otacon will explain the weapon and how it can be used. Some of the conversations are initiated by Otacon or the Colonel, as they call Snake when the player needs to know something about the mission. At other times, if the player gets stuck in a particular part of the game, or if he forgets what the mission objectives are, Snake can contact Otacon or the Colonel. Unfortunately, players cannot ask questions in their own words each time, but generally the advice they receive will get them back on the right path. While *Metal Gear Solid 2* can be a difficult game, the in-game help assists the player in the exploration of the environment.

Perhaps one day libraries can offer a similar help mechanism that automatically detects user frustration and adequately determines the most-likely answer needed to address the situation. Future technological advances may offer smarter catalogs or search interfaces that automatically suggest better search strategies to users who may be struggling with the system. Librarians need not wait for the future invention of smart systems, as there are ways in which librarians can now assist patrons with research in the same manner that Otacon helps Snake defeat the enemy. The easiest way that a librarian can be omnipresent like Otacon is to link chat reference or instant messaging (IM) reference services to every Web page, inside the catalog, and when allowed, inside database interfaces. Chat and IM services can offer immediate point-of-need assistance that patrons can use to solve a problem. Granted, the user must initiate the conversation with a librarian, but he has immediate access to a guide. Conversely, only offering e-mail reference services does not satisfy point-of-need questions, as it takes too long for the librarian to answer the questions. Video games offer help features that instantly give the player feedback and help him figure out a puzzle or defeat an enemy. Similarly, chat and IM offer synchronous communication between the patron and the librarian, allowing the librarian to guide a patron through the research quest with a back-and-forth exchange of questions and answers.

Trial and Error Research

Gamers know that success or mastery of a game means trying and failing many times. In general, gamers do not mind playing the same level over and over again, because they can see the immediate results of their actions. If they use the wrong weapon, take a wrong turn, jump too late or too soon, or miss the critical health pack, they know that they may have to try the level again. However, the goals of the level are generally well defined, as the player can see what is supposed to happen on screen. Conquering an enemy may require timing attacks in a particular sequence, using the appropriate weapon, or attacking in the right places. While this experience can be frustrating, exploration and trial and error eventually lead to success. Getting to the next level, advancing the story, and earning the satisfaction of beating the puzzle are all well-defined incentives for working through the frustration.

Many library patrons may use the same trial and error tactics when conducting research. They may approach a database, type in a few keyword terms or a phrase, hit search, and then see what the system returns. If the system returns nothing, or the results are unsatisfactory, they may alter their search terms to try to get a different results set. Unfortunately, because the search and retrieve functions of a database are not necessarily visible to users, they may not see how their actions influence the search results. When playing a game, users can see exactly what is happening on the screen and can work to correct their actions to be more successful with each attempt. With database searching, the impact of users' actions is not quite as evident, so they may not know how to approach the research situation with a more successful strategy. With each failed search attempt, patrons can grow increasingly frustrated when their trial and error probing of a database fails to yield adequate results. At some point, these patrons may give up, perhaps believing that the database system will not meet their needs, that they are inadequate researchers, or that the system does not work. Such users may eventually ask a librarian for help, but by this time they may be very frustrated. Librarians need to be aware of this trial and error approach to learning and coach patrons through more effective searching. At the same time, the librarian can learn more about what made the patron's previous attempts at the research game unsuccessful, and she can apply that knowledge in developing more user-friendly interfaces, designing library instruction sessions, and conducting reference interviews.

Why Not a Library Video Game?

With an understanding that learning does indeed occur in video games, some librarians are attempting to replicate the success of commercial games and create library video games. Unfortunately, not every library is able to create its own game, as there are barriers. They are costly and resource intensive to produce. Commercial game developers often see making educational games as a risky investment, since they typically do not sell as well as popular video games. Librarians may look at ways to develop games with existing staff and resources, using *Flash*-based game situations. Another option is to modify an existing commercial game by customizing the characters and the environment while still using the game's video engine. This process, called modding, is a way to create a unique game-based experience without having to design a game from the very beginning. With this process, a game modder purchases a licensed copy of a particular video game and uses the video game's engine to run his own version of the game. A game modder will add his own graphics and game assets to the game. Many game publishers are open to modding of their games, because it helps to increase sales. While these options are more affordable than enlisting the services of professional game developers, they do require a great deal of technical expertise. In addition, librarians must be willing to devote significant time and staff resources to the development of a game, and the risks may still outweigh the reward. Many gamers have a negative view of overtly educational games, as they are often (rightly) perceived as an attempt to electrify boring content through a game-based situation. The result is that the game may be viewed as a chore to play rather than a fun learning experience. Librarians and educators are still investigating game-based learning initiatives, and with more experiments we will learn more how video game technologies can be used appropriately to develop engaging library learning experiences.

In the meantime, the most effective way to use game-based learning is by incorporating characteristics from video games into existing or new library services, sources, and instructional efforts. Many librarians are adopting traits from *Google*, *Amazon*, *eBay*, *Wikipedia*, and other popular Web media when redesigning library catalogs and Web sites. Librarians have also been experimenting with blogs, wikis, podcasts, social software, and other applications to get an understanding of how patrons use Web 2.0 tools. This observation and experimentation helps librarians better understand how patrons acquire and use information, how they interact with interfaces, and what they expect from the information seeking experience. Likewise, librarians can learn a great deal from video games, which are becoming one of the most-popular sources of entertainment in our culture. By seeking an understanding of what makes video games such a successful and engaging entertainment medium, librarians can adapt these characteristics to better meet the needs of patrons. Video games offer compelling entertainment experiences that engage those who play them. Video games create an immersive environment for players and encourage them to learn and master the games through exploration and active learning. Librarians also attempt to immerse patrons in their physical and virtual collections while encouraging learning through exploration. They can create a more engaging experience for patrons by observing the successes of video games. This chapter only discusses a few scenarios in which a better understanding of video games can be applied to everyday situations that librarians face. To acquire an even deeper understanding of learning in video games, librarians should observe gamers in action, or even play more games themselves. The experiences learned from video games can be used by librarians to be more effective in meeting the needs of patrons now and in the future.

Sources for Additional Research

Electronic Software Association. 2007. Essential facts about the computer and video game industry. http://www.theesa.com/archives/files/ESA-EF%202007.pdf.

> The Electronic Software Association (http://www.theesa.com) supplies annual sales and demographic data for the video game industry. They provide information about the best-selling video game titles and genres while also offering extensive information about the people who play video games. The ESA also provides other information, including reports that demonstrate how video game sales impact the United States economy.

Gee, J. P. 2004. *What video games have to teach us about learning and literacy*. New York: Palgrave Macmillan.

> James Gee is perhaps one of the best known researchers in the field of educational gaming. This book, written from the perspective of both an educator and a gamer, explores how video games attract players and help them learn. Gee argues that many of the characteristics that make video games successful learning tools need to be adapted to our traditional classroom environment. He believes that the more traditional methods of instruction are not preparing students as well as they should, and that studying video games can help educators offer more effective and relevant classroom instruction.

Glazer, S. 2006. Video games: Do they have educational value? *CQ Researcher* 16 (40).

> In this article, Glazer presents an overview of the debate on the value of games in education. Like most CQ Researcher articles, this one presents two sides to the same argument. Glazer highlights that many researchers believe that gaming can be adapted to educational environments in order to create more engaging learning experiences. She then details the argument that while games are excellent for entertainment purposes, curricular adaptation is impractical and unnecessary.

John C. Beck, M. Wade. 2006. *The kids are alright: How the gamer generation is changing the workplace.* Boston: Harvard Business School Press.

Beck and Mitchell have written this book for executives who will be hiring members of the gamer generation as future employees. Beck and Mitchell argue that while gamers may act and think differently than those who do not play games, managers can leverage many of the strengths of gamers by better understanding them. Gamers may also find the book interesting, as it presents some of the common misconceptions that non-gamer may have about the gamer generation.

Johnson, S. 2006. *Everything bad is good for you: How today's popular culture is actually making us smarter.* New York: Riverhead Books.

While many believe that modern entertainment media is having adverse effects on Americans' level of intelligence, Johnson argues that the reverse is true. In his very convincing argument, Johnson demonstrates how video games, television, and the Internet are increasingly becoming more complicated. As the plots of television shows, the content of the Internet, and the nature of games become more complex, the brains of entertainment consumers are growing and adapting to the changes in media. Johnson dubs this concept the "Sleeper Curve," and demonstrates that Americans' will continue to demand more complicated and engaging entertainment.

Prensky, M. 2006. *"Don't bother me mom, I'm learning!" How computer and video games are preparing your kids for twenty-first century success and how you can help!* St. Paul, MN: Paragon House.

Prensky debunks the popular myth that video games are simply mindless entertainment. He argues that children are actually learning problem solving and other practical skills while playing games. While discussing his point, Prensky defines those who have grown up with video games as "digital natives" and those who have not as "digital immigrants". Throughout the book he offers tips on how parents and educators (digital immigrants) can better understand digital natives.

Van Eck, R. 2006. Digital game-based learning: It's not just the digital natives who are restless. *EDUCAUSE Review* 41 (2): 16-30. http://connect.educause.edu/Library/ EDUCAUSE+Review/DigitalGameBasedLearningI/40614.

Van Eck explores the practicality of integrating video games into classroom instruction. He discusses several different ways of incorporating games, from adapting commercial games to developing new ones to meet curriculum needs. The article addresses the pros and cons of the various methods while also discussing some of the barriers to educational game use.

Works Cited

Electronic Software Association. 2007. *Essential facts about the computer and video game industry.* http://www.theesa.com/archives/files/ESA-EF%202007.pdf.

Gee, J. P. 2004. *What video games have to teach us about learning and literacy.* New York: Palgrave Macmillan.

Graft, K. 2007. Games "will outpace music this year." *Next Generation: Interactive Entertainment Today.* Available from http://www.next-gen.biz/index.php?option=com_co ntent&task=view&id=6094&Itemid=2.

J. C. Beck, M. Wade. 2006. *The kids are alright: How the gamer generation is changing the workplace.* Boston: Harvard Business School Press.

Johnson, S. 2006. *Everything bad is good for you: How today's popular culture is actually making us smarter.* New York: Riverhead Books.

Prensky, M. 2006. *"Don't bother me mom, I'm learning!" How computer and video games are preparing your kids for twenty-first century success and how you can help!.* St. Paul, MN: Paragon House.

CHAPTER 11

From Desk to Web: Creating Safety Nets in the Online Library

Jerilyn R. Veldof

A colleague recently shared a story with me about an interaction she experienced at the reference desk. The patron was a young college student near tears. She had spent hours trying to find enough research to write a paper for her English Composition class and had finally, after many attempts to figure out the library system, come to the reference desk in defeat. She apologized profusely to my colleague, saying that she felt stupid for not being able to find what she needed herself, and that maybe she should not be in school at all.

My colleague did what most of us would do in that situation—rescue the student from distress, restore her sanity, and help renew her faith in the system and herself so that she might come back in the future and try again. The student got the assistance she needed to locate the research that would help her write the paper. That is all well and good, but there is much more potential in this interaction than the application of what is, in the basest sense, merely a band-aid.

Reference librarians have an enormous amount of potential to have a much deeper and broader impact. We encounter a legion of library users through our physical and virtual libraries. These encounters afford us invaluable information that when mined, analyzed, and acted upon can transform the experiences of patrons (like our poor English Composition student) into highly successful, positive, and productive ones.

This chapter is a call to reference and instruction librarians to extend our reach beyond one-to-one encounters and employ our expertise in three ways:

1. To proactively identify and analyze the points in our virtual and physical libraries where users stumble and often give up on the library.

2. To create "safety nets" or support structures at those fail points that gently catch the users and help them on their way.

3. To design more formalized and course integrated e-learning modules that prepare students to navigate and successfully use online resources and services.

Idea of Fail Points

Central to the three roles proposed above is the idea of fail points. To introduce this idea, think back to our English Composition student at the beginning of the chapter. She most likely started her research feeling hopeful. She may have had some good experiences researching papers in the more tightly controlled and highly simplified online environment of her high school media center. Perhaps her past experiences of finding information quickly and successfully in *Google* have helped solidify the notion that research is quick and easy; therefore, the student starts her research with just days to spare before her big paper is due.

It is highly possible, given the density of options on the University of Minnesota Libraries' homepage, that the student feels overwhelmed and panicked at first, but quickly sees the header "Articles and More" and knows to focus on this area of the Web site. However, the links under this header do not make sense to her. What does "Select an Index to Search" mean? She is looking for a text box on the page to search for articles but only sees a search box marked "Books and More." Well, maybe the "more" means articles, so she types in her topic, clicks, and unknowingly encounters her first fail point in the system. Minutes of confusion follow. What is she looking at? What are all of those things on that list? She clicks on some of them, maybe even thinks that some are articles, and tries to figure out how to print them, but there is no print option. She finds a call number, takes that number into the stacks, gets lost because she does not understand how call numbers are arranged, and gives up on finding this item. The student has reached yet another fail point. She goes back to the computer again but this time tries "Select an Index to Search." What she finds on the next page is immediately perplexing. What does an alphabetical list mean? Should she click on the first letter of her topic? She clicks, but the list she is presented with does not make sense. "These aren't articles! This isn't what I want!" With that, the student meets her third fail point.

The story goes on and on. The student tries a different path, gets confused, and goes back. How many times does she repeat this process until she discovers the right path to find an article, finds a person to help her, or gives up entirely? "*Google* is just fine," she declares, and hopes her instructor does not notice the lack of library sources. Giving up entirely, as this student does, represents the "crash and burn" in the illustration below.

Illustration 1 . The Research Process (The Sad Story)

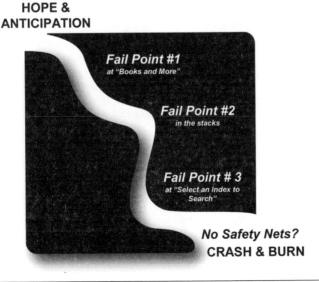

What this student has encountered during her research process is a sequence of fail points—places in the Web site (and/or physical library) that confound, confuse, and puzzle. They are the points at which the user is faced with a dilemma: possibly waste more time trying to figure the system out, search for help on the system, find a friend, colleague, or library employee to help, or—perhaps finally—just give up and leave the library entirely. We likely have no true idea of the number of potential library patrons who do just that—become so disgusted that they discard the library as their source of information and research and go elsewhere.

My guess from having conducted usability testing for over ten years is that this group is sizeable and growing. They do not come to us at our reference desks, they do not e-mail or IM us. Too frequently they have other places to go.

Traditionally we have addressed this group's research challenges by teaching them through in-person or online training. Today, it is even more important to address fail points directly by doing everything we can to eliminate them and to build safety nets so that the fall is minimal, and at worst, a slight annoyance. In this next illustration, the same research story is illustrated, but this time, with safety nets built in.

Illustration 2. The Research Process (The Not-So-Sad Story)

Ferreting Out Fail Points and Building in Safety Nets

The first step in building safety nets is to identify the fail points that necessitate them. Reference librarians are in a unique position to find fail points that patrons encounter in the virtual and physical library. Years of experience answering reference and instructional questions provide librarians with reams of analyzable data on the library's fail points. We need to reflect on the most common research-related questions that reference and instruction librarians get. For example:

- How do I find articles on global warming?
- Does the library own this book that I need to read?

These kinds of questions and the subsequent reference interview begin to reveal the many fail points patrons encounter in the virtual and physical library. There are several levels at which a fail point can occur. I will focus on three levels of fail points; the basic Web usability level, the research process level, and the user's mental models level. The table below correlates the two questions above with these three levels of fail points.

Table 1. Reference Questions Mapped to Fail Points

Question	Fail Points
"How do I find articles on global warming?"	Fail Points at Basic Web Usability Level: "I expect to find something that says "articles" on the homepage. The words "index" or "database" or "periodicals" do not mean anything to me." Fail Points at Research Process Level: "I can't get from point A to B to C. Where are the bridges?" Fail Points at the Mental Model level: "I expect to be able to type my topic in any search box and get articles (whether that be the catalog, in the library's site search box, or in the e-journals list). Is this thing broken?"
Does the library own this book that I need to read?	Fail Points at Basic Web Usability Level: "I expect to find something that says 'books' on this website. The words 'catalog' or 'MNCAT' [the name of the U of MN catalog] do not mean anything to me and I don't see anywhere on this page to go." Fail Points at Research Process Level: "I can't get from point A to B and actually figure out where this book is. The computer says it's here, but I don't know where to go to find it." Fail Points at the Mental Model Level: "I expect that the library would be set-up like the bookstore and I'd just read the signs, go to the right section, and look alphabetically for the author. Why is this so difficult?"

How do we help users overcome these fail points? The first step is to identify these problem areas. There are three main ways to complete this step:

1. Utilize the knowledge of your reference and instruction librarians. They have a richness of experience in guiding people through fail points. Introduce this notion, and ask them to think about questions they frequently receive at the desk and the fail points that those questions indicate. Encourage the librarians to focus on the fail points at all three levels. Follow up with a staff survey or focus group to gather these thoughts. Next, group and rank the fail points in order of frequency so that those with the biggest impact get addressed first.

2. Inventory and analyze the questions received in digital reference and/or in-person reference if that data is available. For example, with over five thousand questions received digitally a year, the University of Minnesota Twin Cities has a rich and varied amount of potential fail points to mine. Minnesota colleagues Houslon, McCready, and Pfahl identified that the category of chat reference questions called "How to find" reflected twenty-seven percent of the total questions received. An analysis of the questions in this category alone has led to the identification of multiple fail points (Houlson, McCready, and Pfahl 2006, 19-39).

3. Mine data from usability tests in which you study where users and systems are failing. Sometimes these problems can be fixed on a structural level, but at other times they are out of the library's control. Although this mining will elicit a wealth of fail points at the basic usability level (Kupersmith 2007, 1), also look for them at the research process and mental models levels.

Given the volume of literature published on library usability in the last ten years, it appears that librarians are getting better at addressing the simpler fail points, such as those created by library terminology or poor Web site design. Fail points at the research process and mental model levels, however, are much more complex and challenging and can not be easily fixed or addressed with a better user interface; reference and instruction librarians are in the best position to provide leadership and expertise in order to address them. The rest of this chapter will address possible Electronic Performance Support System solutions for these types of fail points.

Addressing Research and Mental Model Level Fail Points: Electronic (Library) Performance Support Systems

A key way to help library users successfully navigate through complex systems and processes is by developing Electronic Performance Support Systems (EPSS). EPSSs are, in essence, "safety nets" that can be embedded into other applications to provide support or guidance. They may include tutorials, expert systems, or hyperlinks to reference materials. In the library context, these systems could be interwoven throughout the online library. EPS Systems might appear in the catalog, on the front-end of an SFX menu, or as a stand-alone application that communicates with a database unbeknownst to the student. Key components of EPS Systems might be "unlocked" and reused from existing e-learning tutorials.

Unlocking content from an existing tutorial and repurposing it for use in EPS Systems may be a viable way for libraries to populate EPS Systems that also provides a way for libraries to stretch their e-learning efforts.

An example of commonly used EPSS in the non-library world is tax preparation software. This software anticipates where the tax preparer is likely to encounter fail points and provides safety nets. The tax preparer is alerted to a myriad of deductibles in easy to understand language, given access to interpretations of the tax code, taken through the process, and then given a final product at the end. The tax preparer cannot fail with this system. These EPS Systems do not simulate paper tax forms, nor do they provide tutorials on tax forms. Instead, the software helps you *successfully* fill out your form by taking your metaphorical hand and walking you through the process step-by-step. You learn as you do your task.

Google also understands the importance of preventing user failure. If you misspell something, *Google* provides alternative likely spellings that can avert failure and correct the error. That is a great safety net. *Amazon* is another good example. When you look for a book in *Amazon* but cannot find it, the system suggests two or more books that you did not know you wanted but which satisfy your need. When you end up buying them instead, the safety net becomes a profitable one to *Amazon*.

As with tax software, *Google*, and *Amazon*, we need to build performance support into our library systems in such a way that users cannot fail. Many can be built easily, inexpensively, and with minimal IT assistance. The next section focuses on these small-scale Library Performance Support Systems.

Small-scale Library Performance Support Systems

There are numerous examples of small-scale LPS Systems that pull together relatively basic safety nets that range from simple graphics and terminology to light-weight programming solutions. These safety nets can often be identified during usability evaluations.

The library catalog is a common place of fail points for our users. For example, a simple author search can be a trying experience for users who do not know to enter the author's last name first. The EPSS safety net in this case is the addition of three little words—"last name first"—at the point where the user will see them in the search box. There are numerous other fail points that might be addressed by threading these simple safety nets throughout the catalog to create an LPS "system" that helps the user to search more successfully.

Illustration 3 . Catalog Safety Net

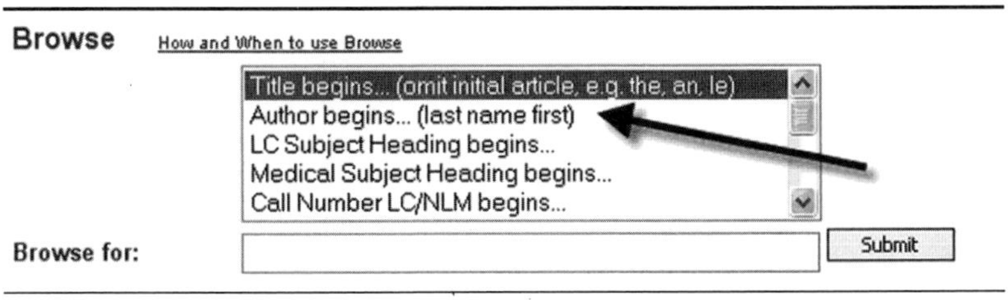

Browse   How and When to use Browse

Title begins... (omit initial article, e.g. the, an, le)
Author begins... (last name first)
LC Subject Heading begins...
Medical Subject Heading begins...
Call Number LC/NLM begins...

Browse for: Submit

The University of Minnesota is experimenting with slightly more advanced components of a catalog LPSS that does not necessitate a change in users' search behavior. When a user types "The" at the beginning of a known title, for example, an invisible program strips the search inquiry of the "the" before the search is executed. The user does not know that the search was ever modified. Likewise, an author search is first executed in the order the user enters it, and then with these search terms reversed.

There are countless other instances of basic safety nets that can be pulled together to create small-scale LPS Systems. For example, during usability testing of the library's homepage at the University of Arizona more than a decade ago, we realized that students did not know what "reference sources" meant and why they would choose them. Likewise, they did not realize that the catalog listed videos and other materials, or that indexes included newspapers, despite the fact that this information was available on the Web site. To correct this disconnect we changed the text-based information to small graphics. Testing proved that these graphics were an excellent safety net for our primary audience of undergraduates.

Illustration 4 . User Interface Safety Net

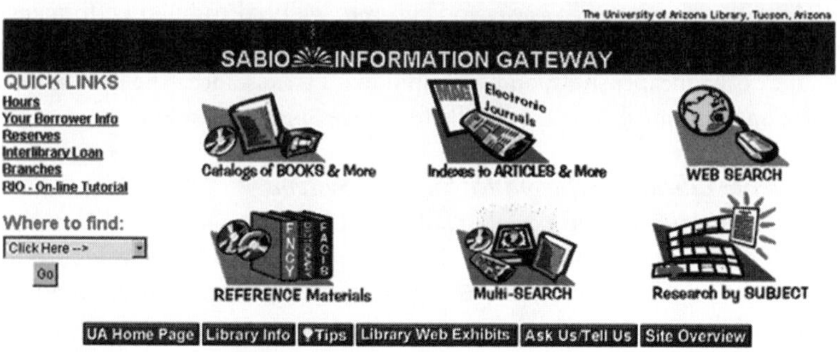

Large-scale Library Performance Support Systems

Large-scale Library Performance Support Systems can be created to act like massive safety nets with smaller Performance Supports embedded within. The tax software discussed earlier is an example. Embedded in this software are features which serve as smaller safety nets (for example, a series of questions that pursue which donations you have made that might be tax deductible).

One example of a large-scale LPSS is the University of Minnesota Libraries' Full-Text Finder. The Full-Text Finder was developed as the result of a process level fail point in which users had difficulty determining if the Libraries had an article that they needed in full-text. The system addressed a mental model fail point at which users did not understand that journal articles can be included in multiple indexes, some with the full-text and some without. Reference and instruction librarians had long noted this fail point through their experiences with confused and frustrated students. We designed the Full-Text Finder to divert users from taking a path where they might encounter multiple fail points. Instead, the FTF directs them towards a tool specifically developed to be a large scale safety net that saves them from a major research and mental model process level fail point.

Illustration 5 . Full Text Finder Initial Box on the University of Minnesota's Undergraduate Virtual Library

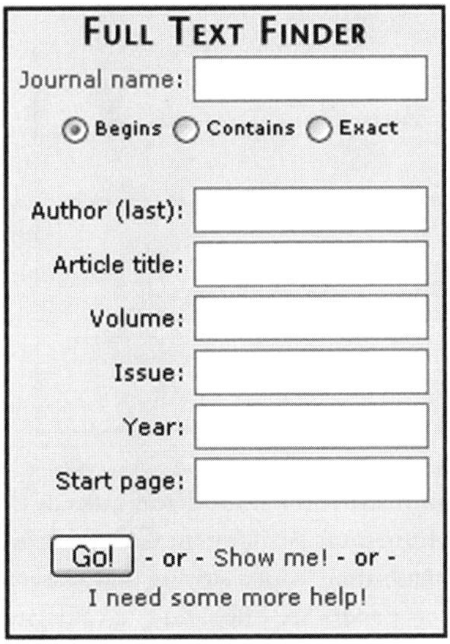

Illustration 6 . Full Text Finder—"Show Me" Interface

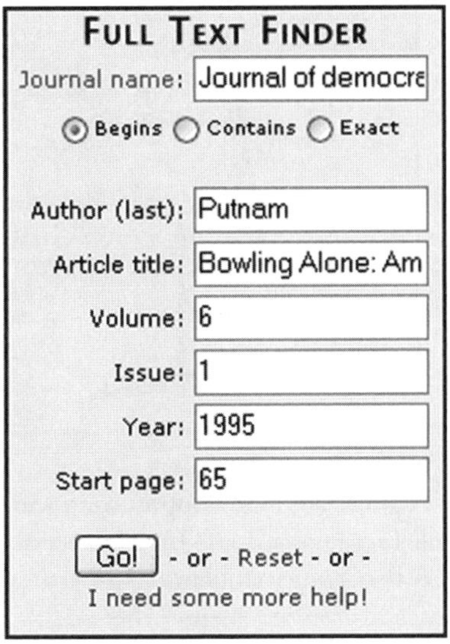

FULL TEXT FINDER

Journal name:

⦿ Begins ◯ Contains ◯ Exact

Author (last):

Article title:

Volume:

Issue:

Year:

Start page:

[Go!] - or - Show me! - or -
I need some more help!

FULL TEXT FINDER

Journal name: Journal of democre

⦿ Begins ◯ Contains ◯ Exact

Author (last): Putnam

Article title: Bowling Alone: Am

Volume: 6

Issue: 1

Year: 1995

Start page: 65

[Go!] - or - Reset - or -
I need some more help!

The Full-Text Finder is featured at the University of Minnesota's Undergraduate Virtual Library (http://www.lib.umn.edu/undergrad/) and appears like this:

An LPSS such as this, however, may also be rife with other potential fail points: Which part of the citation is the article title? What is the name of the journal? Where is the volume number? What if I do not have an issue number? Clearly, citation analysis is a potential fail point. We therefore built multiple safety nets into the Full-Text Finder. Have you hit a fail point because you do not know how to interpret your citation? Click on "Show me" to see an example of the form filled out. Are you still confused? Click on "I need some more help" to go through the process step-by-step (see next illustration). Likewise, if you fill out the form and hit a fail point, the Full-Text Finder sends you into the Full Text Wizard, a step-by-step tool that provides you with an opportunity to try again, this time with examples and point-of-need help.

The Full-Text Finder, therefore, becomes an opportunity to teach students aspects of a citation by giving them the feedback and instruction that they need to correct their own errors. They are motivated to learn because they really are looking for a specific full-text item—not because we have created an artificial learning experience for them (as library tutorials do).

Illustration 7 . Full Text Finder Wizard

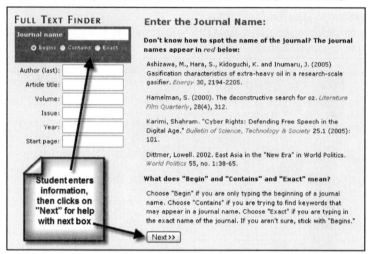

There are many opportunities to wrap instruction around real tasks as the Full Text Finder does. The University of Minnesota's Assignment Calculator is a PSS that guides students step-by-step through their paper writing and research processes. Students enter the date that their papers are due, and the calculator returns specific steps that will help the student to successfully complete the paper on time. The student can receive timed reminders of each step via e-mail. She uses the tool to get just enough help while completing each step. (See illustration 8.) There is also a similar tool designed for the dissertation writing process: the Dissertation Calculator. The Assignment Calculator is accessible from http://www. lib.umn.edu/undergrad/ and the Dissertation Calculator is at http://www.lib. umn.edu/help/disscalc.

Workflow Performance Support Systems

Although building small- and large-scale Library Performance Support Systems is an excellent investment, ultimately we need to find ways to reach our students and faculty where they are working and present Library Performance Support inside that workflow. Lorcan Dempsey, of OCLC, has spent a good deal of time defining this "in the flow" concept for libraries. Using his model, we adapt to users' current workflows and help them to do their work there, instead of forcing them to temporarily engage in library spaces disconnected from their workflows (Dempsey 2006). A student's natural workflow might be in their course site, the writing center's site, or in other systems that we build to help them get their work done. A library presence in student workflow reflects the ultimate Library Performance Support System.

Illustration 8. The Assignment Calculator

ASSIGNMENT CALCULATOR
YOU CAN BEAT THE CLOCK!

Want to try a different date?
Start Date: 6 - 22 - 2007
Due Date: [ ] - [ ] - 2007

Starting on: 6/22/2007
Ending on: 8/21/2007
According to the dates you have entered, you have 59 days to finish.

Re-Calculate Schedule!

Submit for email reminders!

STEP 1   By Sun Jun 24, 2007: Understand your assignment
• Suggestions for understanding assignment sheets

STEP 2   By Tue Jun 26, 2007: Select and focus topic
• Refine your topic
• How to begin

STEP 3   By Wed Jun 27, 2007: Write working thesis
• Definition: Thesis Statements and Research Questions
• Sample thesis statements

STEP 4   By Fri Jun 29, 2007: Design research strategy
• QuickStudy: Designing a research strategy
• AskUs at the Libraries can also help

STEP 5   By Wed Jul 04, 2007: Find, review, and evaluate books
• Keep careful notes, with source clearly indicated
• Search the library's catalog
• QuickStudy: Finding Books

STEP 6   By Thu Jul 19, 2007: Find, review, and evaluate journal/magazine/newspaper articles
• Keep careful notes, with source clearly indicated
• QuickStudy: Finding Articles
• Research QuickStart

STEP 7   By Mon Jul 23, 2007: Find, review, and evaluate web sites
• Do some general web searching - not Library-related
• Keep careful notes, with source clearly indicated
• QuickStudy: Finding web sites
• Research QuickStart

STEP 8   By Tue Jul 24, 2007: Outline or describe overall structure
• Starting a Writing Project
• Using Outlines
• Center for Writing

STEP 9   By Mon Jul 30, 2007: Write 1st draft
• Writing Your First Draft
• Center for Writing
• Reserve computer lab time on the Lab Reservation System

STEP 10   By Sun Aug 05, 2007: Conduct additional research as necessary
• QuickStudy: Evaluating Sources
• 'Ask Us' at the University Libraries

STEP 11   By Fri Aug 17, 2007: Revise & rewrite
• Revising Your Work
• Online or In-person writing instruction at the U of MN's Center for Writing

STEP 12   By Tue Aug 21, 2007: Put paper in final form
• QuickStudy: Citing Sources
• The Elements of Style - William Strunk, Jr.
• RefWorks: Citing sources using an online tool

There are plenty of opportunities for LPSS that are "in the flow" of our users and can help them actually get their work done (just as the TaxAct program does for taxpayers). What if the Assignment Calculator, for example, was a full-service tool in which students wrote their papers and did their research? It could bring together word processing capabilities, citation software, and metasearch functionality. Help from instructors, librarians, writing consultants, or fellow students could be provided from within the Assignment Calculator at the point and level of need.

An example of this kind of LPSS that is waiting funding for further development is another Minnesota tool currently called "My Field." (See illustration 9.) My Field breaks down the researcher's process into four areas as illustrated in this screen shot. The LPSS then provides researchers with tools that support each of these areas; discovery research, gathering research, creating new

Illustration 9 . My Field

works, and sharing them with others. The Libraries will embed library help, instruction, and support through and around these areas and tools, creating various levels of safety nets throughout.

Leveraging Tutorial Content for Library Performance Support Systems

There is still an important educational role for formal e-learning tutorials in libraries despite the potency of LPS Systems to address fail points. A tutorial (or classroom situation), for example, is better suited to address deep-seated mental models of the research process, such as:

- The user who has a Mental Model of research as a quick process where *Google* may be used to find Web pages supporting his or her argument.
- The user who has a Mental Model of the library as a free bookstore similar to Borders or Barnes & Noble.

Libraries, however, should not have to fully staff and fund two separate efforts—one to build online tutorials and another to build Library Performance Support Systems. Instead, online tutorials should be built so that content can be repurposed into Library Performance Support Systems. In this way the time and resources invested in building both online tutorials and LPSS can be more wisely leveraged.

There are three basic building blocks for designing online tutorial content that can be repurposed into Library Performance Support Systems. The first building block concerns learning objects.

Learning Objects

Learning objects are discrete learning tools that can be mixed-and-matched in various learning venues and contribute to the development of Library Performance Support Systems. Examples include a streaming video that demonstrates a keyword search, or short exercises that provide users with feedback on their ability to identify the key words in a sample research topic. Learning objects can also be as low-tech as a handout with screen captures and instructions.

Learning objects can be repurposed and delivered to multiple targets within the library site as well as into external systems (such as course or department pages and writing center tools and support). Learning objects can also be grouped to provide traditional e-learning in the form of tutorials, but unbundle these learning objects and *voilà*, you have bite-sized content for embedding into both small- and large-scale LPSS.

Once engaged in a learning object, the user should be given the flexibility to complete his task (e.g. find a call number he actually needs) or to move into a tutorial module with more robust instruction. In order to accomplish this kind of mobility, the library's performance support needs to be scaffolded so that educational components become paths into more—or less—content.

Illustration 10. Library's Performance Support Pyramid

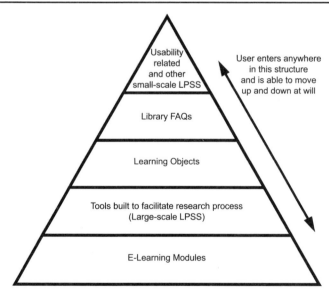

This may sound daunting. How can we really make it work? You can imagine multiple small-scale and large-scale performance support systems with pages and pages of supporting content. Every time the library changes (or eliminates) the OPAC or key databases, for example, we would have to modify multiple pages of help, instruction, and support that refer to the OPAC or database. What librarians need to successfully manage learning objects are special databases that hold these learning objects. This leads to the second building block for creating online tutorials that also support LPSS—Learning Content Management Systems.

Learning Content Management Systems

Learning Content Management Systems are like storage systems for learning objects. Instead of having an interactive exercise on call number order located in various places and servers across the library system, one interactive product resides in the Learning Content Management System and is delivered to multiple online targets. Many libraries have similarly employed library content databases that drive link and descriptions to licensed databases to various library Web pages (see the LibData model at http://libdata.sourceforge.net/ for an example). A library tutorial would need a similar kind of content management system that would drive learning objects to various LPSS targets.

Authoring Tools

The third building block for creating online tutorials that support LPS Systems revolves around authoring tools that assist librarians in creating interactive learning objects. Full-scale authoring tools such as Trivantis' *Lectora* provide plug-and-play ability to create quizzes, mix-and-match interactives, and more. Other, more specific, authoring tools (such as *Camtasia* and *Captivate*) assist the developer in creating screencasts, building interactive exercises (as with *Flash*), creating quizzes (as with *Survey Monkey*), or designing games (as with *Game Show Presenter*) and graphics (as with *Adobe Illustrator*).

These three building blocks are key for repurposing tutorial content into LPS Systems. In addition to these building blocks there are several other layers of capability that could also be added:

• Capacity for integrating individual components (or "reusable learning objects") into other venues (such as *WebCT*, Assignment Calculators, e-portfolios, FAQs, and various Web sites including those outside the library). This would allow libraries to more easily provide instruction, support, and quick tips wherever users might need it.

• Capacity to track learners' use of learning objects wherever they encounter them and provide instructor/faculty reports.

• Capacity to use and integrate learning objects created from multiple authoring tools (e.g. *Camtasia*, *Illustrator*, and *Flash*).

• Capacity to customize authoring so that various librarians can create unique modules for plug-and-play use and integrate them into pathfinders, academic departmental Web sites, etc.

By incorporating these building blocks and some of the above capacities into new tutorial development, reference and instruction librarians can avoid the duplication and unwieldiness of having the same content replicated at numerous fail points. They can also create more robust LPS Systems that interrelate seamlessly with their online tutorials.

Conclusion

The effort to identify fail points and to design effective Library Performance Support Systems that address them can be a daunting enterprise. However, libraries should not continue to treat large-scale, glaring fail points with mere "band-aids." Library users rely more and more on the virtual library, reference desk traffic is slowing, and these trends may lead to a reduction in hiring. As the Web continues to develop, the future of the reference librarian may become even more marginal to the success of our current, and potential, library users.

If librarians want to continue to provide access to quality materials and to give a high-level of assistance at the reference desk, they also need to ensure that fail points are proactively identified and that problems are addressed as much as possible at their source. This proactive approach amounts to building a robust, effective, and far-reaching "virtual reference desk" made up of the kinds of safety nets and support structures discussed in this chapter. By expanding the role of the reference librarian in this way, we ensure both the survival of the position and its centrality to the future success of our users.

Sources for Additional Research

Brown, L. A. 1996. *Designing and developing electronic performance support systems.* Boston: Digital Press.
> There are several books on building Performance Support Systems. This one discusses a commonly used model for instructional design that includes these steps: Define, Design, Develop, and Deliver.

Carliner, S. 2002. Considerations for designing electronic performance support systems. *Technical Communication* 49 (4): 411.
> This article is written for practitioners in the technical communications field and is therefore very applicable to those developing Library Performance Support Systems. Carliner differentiates between high-level performance support design and what he calls detailed design, and offers practical advice at each design step.

Clark, R. C. 1998. Recycling knowledge with learning objects. *Training & Development* 52 (10): 60-63.
> Clark clearly explains learning objects and the ways they can, and should, be repurposed. She also discusses the importance of organizing and tagging these objects.

Gery, G. 1991. *Electronic performance support systems: How and why to remake the workplace through the strategic application of technology.* Boston: Weingarten Publications.
> This is the book that introduced the Performance Support System concept. The reality may not have matched up to this ideal, but Gery's book is still worth a read.

Maughan, G. R. 2005. Electronic performance support systems and technological literacy. *Journal of Technology Studies* 31 (1): 49-56.
> This article is a compelling argument to use Performance Support Systems to facilitate use of challenging technologies. It includes a section on embedding performance support in the user's workflow.

Van Schaik, P., P. Barker, and O. Famakinwa. 2006. Potential roles for performance support tools within library systems. *Electronic Library* 24 (3): 347-365.

This article from the UK describes a stand-alone Performance Support System designed to help students use the library classification system in order to locate the books that they need. A study on its effectiveness concluded that the students found the system useful, but that changes and improvements were recommended.

Van Schaik, P., R. Pearson, and P. Barker. (2002). Designing electronic performance support systems to facilitate learning. *Innovations in Education & Teaching International* 39 (4): 289-306.

This article describes a stand-alone Performance Support System designed to help psychology students use SPSS, a statistical software program. The section on integrating help is of particular interest to librarians.

Works Cited

Dempsey, L. 2006. The (digital) library environment: Ten years after. *Ariadne* 46. http://www.ariadne.ac.uk/issue46/dempsey/.

Houlson, V., K. McCready, and C. Steinberg Pfahl. 2006. A Window into our patron's needs: Analyzing data from chat transcripts. *Internet Reference Services Quarterly* 11 (4): 19-39.

Kupersmith, J. Library terms that users understand. http://www.jkup.net/terms.html.

CHAPTER 12

Be You; Be Unique: How to Create Competitive Reference Services by Being Strategically Different

Jill S. Stover

A company surrenders today's businesses when it gets smaller faster than it gets better. A company surrenders tomorrow's businesses when it gets better without getting different.
~ Gary Hamel, author and consultant

As any drummer marching to his own beat will say, being different is good. In the library marketing world, being different is even better when those differences result in an appealing competitive advantage. Even though the library's reference desk operates in a non-profit environment, it too needs points of differentiation to thrive. In fact, being strategically different is an absolute necessity for libraries that compete in an increasingly overcrowded marketplace where Internet search engines, information service providers, and even coffee shops vie for patrons' attention. To achieve strategic differentiation, academic reference librarians must implement competitive marketing strategies at every stage of their service planning—from the earliest brainstorming sessions, to implementation, and finally, to promotion and assessment. This chapter will discuss what it means to be different from a marketing standpoint, why being different is important, and how to achieve a sustainable competitive advantage through the differentiation of reference services. In doing so, reference librarians can secure their place in patrons' lives well into the future.

What's the Difference?

The Merriam-Webster dictionary defines the word "different" as "partly or totally unlike in nature, form, or quality," "not the same as." This broad definition hardly does justice to the strategy and creativity involved in constructing meaningful, differentiated services that compel patrons to take notice and, in the end, choose your reference services over competitors'. For librarians, it is not enough to simply be different from other information service providers. Reference services must be different with respect to the qualities that matter most to patrons. Marketer Robert Fisher explains differentiation this way: "Differentiation is achieved when consumers perceive that a service differs from competitive offerings on any characteristic, including price. Differentiation is based on aspects of the service that are salient to consumers and ultimately have a favorable influence on their preferences" (1991, 19). In other words, there are two main components of successful differentiation. First, patrons must be able to recognize that a service is, in fact, distinct from the competition. Second, patrons must care about that difference. If both of these criteria are fulfilled, then differentiation can be wielded as a competitive advantage.

As consultant Jaynie Smith defines it, a competitive advantage is "what separates you from the rest of the herd. It's what keeps your business alive and growing. In short, it's the reason you're in business" (2006, 1). Being different, then, is not an end unto itself. By identifying and capitalizing on what makes services different and superior to others, librarians can insure the current and future health of their reference services while creating real value for patrons.

Just like every other facet of marketing, a differentiation strategy is subject to change. As new competitive threats emerge and patrons' demands evolve, competitive advantages must be reevaluated, and new differentiators will need to be developed and/or highlighted. Recall that patrons are the final judge as to whether a competitive advantage is achieved, a determination they make according to the attributes they value and the alternatives available. Developments in the competitive landscape and consumer preferences will alter how patrons perceive library services and, in turn, how librarians choose to distinguish themselves. In order to keep up with these changes and remain relevant, it is crucial to monitor consumer trends, the competition, and a library's internal status regularly—topics that will be addressed later in this chapter.

Why Be Different?

Differentiation is a competitive act. Holding a unique, noteworthy position in the marketplace requires knowing enough about oneself and one's competitors so that you can demonstrate how you are distinct from and better than the rest. In turn, resulting competitive advantages enable librarians to draw patrons away from other organizations and services so that they can benefit from reference offerings. For many librarians, who value cooperation and collaboration, the very thought of competing in this way is anathema, but it need not be so. In fact, competition is a necessary and beneficial undertaking common to all organizations, including nonprofits. In his book concerning nonprofit competition, *Play to Win*, David La Piana argues that competition is a serious ethical duty. He states,

> I came to believe that it is the responsibility of effective nonprofits…to do everything in their power to attract the resources they need to continue and expand their work. This includes, when the opportunity arises, winning resources away from less effective nonprofits through an ethical yet aggressive strategy that differentiates them from the pack of those offering similar services. This competitive imperative is driven by my belief that the mission of any nonprofit is…to effect change, advance the nonprofit's social mission, and in the end actually make the world, or at least a small part of it, a better place. (2005, 13)

Distinguishing reference services so that patrons can understand their usefulness and apply them to their goals is competitive, but it is also a healthy behavior for any library and a benefit to users. Competition should be embraced as a means of making services effective in addressing patrons' needs.

There are also other, equally practical reasons for adopting a competitive stance within a reference department. If you have not done so in a while, take a stroll around your campus. If it is like most, you will be hard-pressed to find a flat surface unadorned by promotional materials of one form or another, never mind the sponsored advertisements found on Web sites and on television. According to some estimates, the average American consumer is exposed to an astounding three thousand marketing messages per day (Casison-Tansiri 2007, 1). Those consumers are also patrons, and librarians must compete for their attention among thousands of organizations. How can reference librarians cut through this massive amount of clutter if their services do not stand out from the crowd? Avoiding this question in service planning can result in patrons overlooking the very services intended to benefit them.

Finally, the information marketplace is home to an ever-increasing number of service providers who directly target patrons with products that substitute for academic library reference services. Competitive intelligence expert Cynthia Cheng Correia describes this current situation by stating, "Today, competition in our profession and related industries tends to be more clearly defined and threats tend to be greater. We have witnessed the ensuing fallout on too many libraries and information centers as we face non-traditional competition" (2006, 24). Cheng and others (Bell 2002, Davidson 1999, Flower 2004, Gibbons 2001) cite search engines (such as *Google*), online services aimed directly at end users (such as *Questia*, *XanEdu*, and *ebrary*), and content management systems (such as *Blackboard*) as new threats to the supremacy of the academic library. In addition to luring people away from the reference desk, these services also alter patrons' expectations, particularly regarding the amount the time that they will spend acquiring quality information. Librarian Virginia Massy-Burzio argues, "If we wish to survive in the future, we need to challenge old philosophies and be much more responsive to user needs. In the Internet environment, we will have to fight to keep our users and not only offer them the collections and services they need and want, but also provide it to them quickly and conveniently" (2002, 775). Traditional sources of competition, such as peer recommendations, will also exert greater influence within the competitive landscape as online social networks become more prevalent and make it increasingly easy for patrons to seek assistance from trusted classmates or colleagues rather than their campus librarians.

If current trends extend into the future, librarians will face even more competition from information service providers. These competitors wield sufficient resources to precisely target markets within academia and advertise directly to patrons, while offering them customized, easy-to-use products that are viable alternatives to reference services. The future sustainability of those services will rely on librarians' ability to deploy their assets to provide patrons with benefits unmatched by competitors, and then to utilize and communicate those points of differentiation as a competitive advantage. The best defense against future threats is to think offensively about how to become strategically different. Libraries must discover innovative ways to realize their libraries' missions and strategic plans, and to brandish those strengths to delight patrons. The next sections will describe how to determine what makes reference services unique, and how to leverage those differences throughout service planning.

Keep Competitors Close

Academic reference librarians face competition on many different fronts. Competition could come in the form of Internet search engines that harried patrons turn to for last-minute research papers, or coffee shops where student groups go to caffeinate for late night study sessions, or information service providers that promote themselves directly to teaching faculty. Competition can even arise from ineffective programs that drain resources from more fruitful endeavors. For example, devoting scarce time and personnel to projects that are no longer effective can detract from libraries' ability to respond to changing demands. In order to successfully counter competitive threats, one must first identify who the closest competitors are and the specific threat they pose. It is not useful or practical to focus on every conceivable competitor, but one must target those that are the most threatening. Talking to patrons and non-users and observing their behaviors will provide clues as to who is luring them away from library services. Also, frontline staff can help to identify the most pressing competitors.

Depending on the nature of the competitive threat, librarians can find competitive information from a myriad of external sources as well:

- Organizational Web sites and publications
- Word-of-mouth
- Professional organizations and presentations
- Trade journals and industry reports
- Newspapers and magazines
- Weblogs and social networks

One of the best ways to investigate competitors is to patronize their services. There is no better strategy for fully understanding the appeal of another organization than to experience what it is like to use its services firsthand.

After identifying the closest competitors, one must determine the type of threat they present to reference services. Do they compete with libraries for funding, reference interactions, media attention, or other resources? By understanding the exact nature of the threat posed, librarians can devise focused strategies for countering them. For instance, if you find that students look for answers to research questions by visiting the social networking site *Facebook* because they enjoy its online communication features, you can investigate how to increase your reference transactions by incorporating social networking features into your Web pages.

To Thine Own Self Be True

There are a few cardinal marketing sins one would do well to avoid in constructing a competitive advantage. One is to promise patrons things that cannot be delivered. It is important to conduct a realistic assessment of what can and cannot be provided and be honest with patrons about those limitations. Therefore, it is not advisable to simply copy another organization's differentiation strategy. On the other hand, librarians must not waste opportunities because they either ignore or underestimate their service strengths. Another equally damaging mistake is to become so consumed with competing and "one-upping" other organizations that a library's core identity is lost. Even the best marketers can make this mistake, as evidenced by Starbucks Chairman Howard Schultz's recent internal memo to executives warning that the company strayed too far from its original purpose. In the memo, Schultz expressed his desire that the company refocus on its primary role—purveyor of specialty coffees (Adamy 2007, sec. A). Libraries, after all, are libraries. As such, they hold a special position within society. References services, therefore, should not merely mimic the latest competitive offerings, but rather, they should reflect each library's unique capabilities and special benefits.

To avoid possible pitfalls, begin forming a competitive strategy by analyzing the reference department's strengths and weaknesses. Many groups engaged in strategic thinking, strategic planning, or marketing use the common environmental analysis, SWOT, to accomplish this task. SWOT is an acronym that stands for Strengths, Weaknesses, Opportunities, and Threats. Note that strengths and weaknesses are internal and relate to circumstances within the department or library. Opportunities and threats, on the other hand, refer to developments in the external environment, such as economics, funding, vendor behavior, etc. In addition, be sure to consider SWOT elements relative to competitors. If you find that you and your competitors share the same strengths, consider how you apply them differently and whether your approach has some relative advantage over the others.

In assessing strengths and weaknesses, consider your abilities in the following areas as starting points. List strengths and weaknesses as they pertain to:

• Relationships	• Special areas of expertise
• Responsiveness	• Awards/Recognitions
• Reputation	• Programs
• Patron satisfaction/Preference	• Efficiency
• Purpose (Mission)	• Technology/Web presence
• Service availability	• Collections
• Funding	• Creativity/Innovation
• Promotions/Communication channels	• Bureaucracy

While the bulk of this work can be completed internally, consider inviting select patrons and other stakeholders to review the list. As outsiders, they are likely to think of strengths and weaknesses that you have not considered.

Next, discover the opportunities and threats emerging on campus and elsewhere. Again, opportunities and threats often originate outside the reference department, but they can have a substantial impact on it. Threats can be found on campus, in the local community, or in the general marketplace. Another analytical tool, PEST, is helpful in this process. PEST is a mnemonic tool to remind groups to look at Political, Environmental, Social, and Technological factors that influence opportunities and threats. For example, the introduction of the *iPod* changed the way people consume music, thereby posing a threat to some in the music industry, but it also opened up some opportunities for librarians to explore podcasting as an outreach and instructional tool. Monitoring government reports, newspapers, magazines, and Web logs is useful in keeping up-to-date with these factors. For instance, Web sites such as *TrendWatching* and *TrendCentral* report on important consumer trends, while *Gizmodo* and *Engadget* discuss the latest consumer technologies.

Identifying opportunities is a largely creative exercise because it involves imagining new ways in which services can be put to use as well as identifying openings in sectors of the environment. An opportunity, as it is defined here, is a chance to develop reference services to address an unmet or underserved need. Opportunities can take any number of forms, including new campus-wide initiatives, curriculum changes, new acquisition or application of technology, changes in consumer behaviors or preferences, library-friendly faculty, and so on. Often, opportunities take the guise of threats, so be sure that your staff examines all angles of a situation to uncover hidden opportunities. A competitive reference librarian is always seeking opportunities to serve patrons in unexpected ways. Indeed, the ability to spot such opportunities can be a competitive advantage of sorts. Fortunately, since academic librarians are embedded in their campus communities, they are well-positioned to spot opportunities that are exclusive to their institutions.

After a thorough review of opportunities, consider the threats to the department. Threats are conditions that possess the potential to undermine library goals and the ability to serve patrons effectively. Certainly, budget cuts can be threatening, but so too can negative word-of-mouth. Examining weaknesses to understand their underlying causes can reveal potential threats.

Table 1. SWOT Matrix

	Strengths	Weaknesses
Opportunities	Apply strengths to opportunities.	Address weaknesses so as to take advantage of key opportunities.
Threats	Use strengths to counter threats.	Bolster weaknesses to defend against serious threats.

A SWOT analysis is incomplete until all of these elements are paired in what is known as a SWOT Matrix. The Matrix reveals how strengths can be used to capture opportunities while compensating for weaknesses. The following is a SWOT Matrix with accompanying strategies:

Beyond SWOT: Being Strategically Different

The SWOT Analysis enables librarians to form a realistic picture of the environment and of how they compare in the marketplace and what their capabilities are, but it does little to elucidate how they should proceed to secure a strategically different position in patrons' minds. If SWOT indicates what path to follow, strategic differentiation offers a means of getting there. In fact, many of your competitors have probably completed a SWOT Analysis and have come to conclusions much like your own. The distinctive and creative methods librarians use to implement the SWOT findings, however, can propel them ahead of competitors and allow them to stand out and be noticed. The remainder of this chapter outlines marketing approaches that you can employ to find your distinct niche within your academic community.

Being dramatically different is the theme of Marty Neumeier's inspiring book, *Zag: The Number-One Strategy of High-Performance Brands*. In it, Neumeier asserts that successful brands must penetrate consumers' increasingly resilient mental barriers to marketing clutter by being radically different from alternatives. To achieve radical differentiation, he suggests finding what he calls the "white space," or open market space (2007, 40). Locating these market niches requires the ability to see what is absent from your campus and imagine ways that you can fill in those gaps. The following sections include strategies for exposing unmet needs in campuses' white spaces.

Reconsider Your Segmentation Strategy

One way to unearth differentiation ideas is to take a fresh look at the groups of patrons, or market segments, the library serves. Market segments are groups of people (patrons) who respond similarly to service offerings. In academic libraries, most librarians divide their patrons according to their academic rank (freshman, graduate student, etc.), status (student, faculty, staff), and discipline. While this segmentation strategy might be the most simple, it is a poor foundation for constructing innovative reference service strategies. Segmenting patrons in these ways presumes that all sophomore Biology majors will be served equally well by the same suite of offerings, which is, of course, untrue. There are, however, other creative options for grouping patrons so that they can be served better by unique service offerings.

Both Neumeier and marketing experts Clayton Christensen, Scott Cook, and Taddy Hall agree that to achieve differentiation and innovation, organizations ought to focus on the jobs that people want to get done, rather than on their customers' demographic characteristics. As Christensen, Cook, and Hall explain in their article, "Marketing Malpractice: The Cause and the Cure," marketers go awry when they base their product designs on customer types:

There is a better way to think about market segmentation and new product innovation. The structure of a market, seen from the customers' point of view, is very simple: They just need to get things done...The marketer's task is therefore to understand what jobs periodically arise in customers' lives for which they might hire products the company could make. If a marketer can understand the job, design a product and associated experiences in purchase and use to do that job, and deliver it in a way that reinforces its intended use, then when customers find themselves needing to get that job done, they will hire that product. (2005, 76)

The same is true of patrons—they do not come to the library wanting books and articles. They come wanting to write English papers, complete research projects, investigate grants, decide which stocks to purchase, and so on. Library materials are a means, not an end. To develop remarkable reference services, therefore, librarians must recognize what patrons wish to accomplish and where the library fits in the process of achieving their goals. Then, librarians can customize reference services to assist patrons in completing their jobs, rather than just locating the raw materials needed to get them done.

Consider this example of how creative segmentation could impact reference services: librarians realize that an increasing number of students on their campus are required to give oral presentations as part of their coursework, but many of them have little experience speaking in front of groups and constructing presentations. To tend to this unmet need, reference librarians approach university departments requesting support for co-sponsoring training sessions on how to create and deliver presentations. The departments and librarians work together to identify practitioners in the students' fields of interest to co-teach the sessions, while librarians gather the resources for background information on effective presentation skills and set aside library space as a designated presentation practice area. Librarians also create a supplemental Web portal on the topic where they post sample presentations, *PowerPoint* user guides, helpful Web sites, and streaming video examples. As a result, librarians become the de facto campus authority on presentation help and support, thereby differentiating themselves as the only service providers to offer this kind of help. This one-of-a-kind service garners attention and praise from faculty, who do not have the class time to train students on presenting, but nevertheless want to augment their skills. They enthusiastically promote the library's training sessions to students in their courses, which defends against future competitors who might otherwise choose to offer similar services.

Researchers Kim and Mauborgne (1999) agree that to compete in today's congested marketplace, organizations must construct new "market space" by looking at familiar assumptions, including assumptions about target customers, from a fresh perspective. In their article, "Creating New Market Space," they summarize six strategies for competing by re-envisioning the market. One strategy involves redefining organizations' conceptions of who the target customer is. They state, "Challenging an industry's conventional wisdom about which buyer group to target can lead to the discovery of new market space" (88). On an academic campus, for example, it may be best to target parents in some instances, rather than students directly, in order to increase the undergraduates' usage of library services.

Build Networks

In the previous presentation training example, librarians sought cooperation from departments and local professionals. Building a strong network of connections on and off campus that works to deliver value to patrons can be an effective approach to distinguishing services. Joining with local community organizations, for instance, can offer insights into community issues as well as personal connections. These insights can be utilized in working with patrons researching local topics, for example. Developing specialized areas of knowledge and social networks are difficult for others to duplicate and may result in a competitive advantage. Many academic librarians build beneficial relationships with campus units such as writing centers, academic integrity offices, and student services, to name a few.

Librarians should also seek partnerships with the people they serve—their patrons. As with any service, patrons and librarians must work together to create a positive outcome and a pleasant experience. By recognizing this reality and forming strong bonds with patrons, librarians can make their reference services more satisfying and relevant, and thereby more competitive. As some marketing researchers say, "One opportunity for organizations to compete through service is to identify innovative ways of co-creating value. Interactivity and doing things with the customer versus doing things to the customer is the hallmark of S-D [service-dominant] logic" (Lusch, Vargo, and O'Brien 2007, 11). Reference librarians, then, should invite patrons to take part in service planning, development, and delivery from the bottom up, so that they have a personal stake in those services. In turn, the patrons' investments in those reference services will distinguish them from other competitive offerings.

Other librarians embrace the competition as allies. The Western Kentucky University Libraries sponsor a lecture series that takes place at the local Barnes & Noble bookstore. Still many other libraries participate in the *Google Scholar Library Links* project whereby patrons can discover local library resources in their search results through the institution's link resolver. In each case, the libraries' integrity and unique purpose is preserved and entrenched through its network of connections, making it difficult to uproot their position as competition intensifies. Such differentiators are most effective when the connections serve to make patrons' experiences more rich and rewarding.

Excel at Service

When asked what makes their services better than anyone else's, it is likely that most librarians would respond that they deliver outstanding customer service.

While this assertion sounds like an advantage, it is much like the claims that most service providers make. Instead of "outstanding," organizations may use words such as excellent, superior, and quality, but they are equally vague, subjective, and ultimately, indistinguishable. To truly set services apart, consultant Jaynie Smith recommends in her book, *Creating Competitive Advantage*, that marketers be specific about their organizations' accomplishments. Smith asserts that competitive advantages should be:

1. Objective
2. Quantifiable
3. Not claimed by competitors
4. Not clichés (2006, 21-22)

When attempting to specify advantages, quantify indicators beyond reference transactions to capture those statistics that are most meaningful to various patron audiences. Smith suggests that "the key is to focus not simply on your product/service itself, but on all aspects of your relationship with your customer. Every one of your deliverables offers an opportunity for a competitive advantage or competitive positioning" (2006, 113). Such examples could include:

- Referrals to your services
- Turnaround times
- Relative service hours
- Satisfaction rates
- Partnering organizations
- Special training or education

In exploring what makes your services stand out, it is important to ask patrons which service qualities they value the most. There is no point in promoting points of differentiation that patrons do not recognize as significant.

Make Small Things Count Big

It is not always necessary to restructure the entire host of reference services to attain a differentiated status. Sometimes small changes in how librarians interact with patrons can enhance prominence. Consider the following example from a popular fast-food restaurant, Chick-fil-A. Chick-fil-A is highly differentiated by its religious underpinnings, as articulated in its mission statement, "to glorify God by being a faithful steward of all that is entrusted to us and to have a positive influence on all who come in contact with Chick-fil-A" (Chick-fil-A 2007). The company expresses its mission by being closed on Sundays and by investing in character-building children's programming. It also achieves its mission in more subtle ways. For example, when customers thank Chick-fil-A employees, they respond not with the ordinary and expected "you're welcome," but with the memorable and polite words, "my pleasure." This tiny adjustment to the status quo sets them apart from their competitors while holding true to their mission of being a "positive influence" on their customers by making them feel valued.

Likewise, librarians should utilize points of contact with patrons as chances to express their own special vision and values. Marketing expert Peter Fisk calls this vision the "big idea that defines you" in his book, *Marketing Genius*. He says that powerful brands "connect companies with people, both emotionally and practically and, most importantly, by ensuring the promises become realities over time" (2006, 152). In your interactions with patrons, imagine how you can incorporate your professional ethos and library character into the transaction. Simply modifying your phone greeting, sending thank you notes, following-up on questions, surprising people with gift cards, and adding interactive elements to your Web site are all venues to convey your sincerity and professionalism.

Showing up in unexpected contexts is another option for differentiating your services. Librarian David Fulton of the Liverpool Public Library in New York has had some success providing reference services to patrons at local Panera Bread restaurants as described in his blog, *Daveman's Tech Tips* (Fulton 2006). Such efforts increase librarians' visibility, add extra convenience, and demonstrate librarians' relevance in a myriad of circumstances. They also provide patrons with something extraordinary to talk about with their peers.

Conclusion

Marketing guru Seth Godin proclaims in his popular book, *Purple Cow*, that "remarkable marketing is the art of building things worth noticing right into your product or service. Not slapping on marketing as a last-minute add-on, but understanding if your offering isn't remarkable, it's invisible" (2003, 3). As the future unfolds for libraries, the need to be strategically different, or remarkable, is ever more pressing. Competition will only continue to increase, and other organizations will become savvier in reaching campus constituents. If reference services do not deliver value that is clearly distinct from and superior to alternatives, there is no reason for reference librarians to remain in business. As Godin says, a sound, competitive marketing strategy with a focus on differentiation is a must for any service provider who does not want to get lost in the crowd.

Planning for differentiation in reference services should be strategic, not accidental. As discussed is this chapter, there are four steps in achieving strategic differentiation:

1. Adopt a competitive mindset.
2. Know your department, your library, your competitors, and your patrons, and be aware of what you can reasonably offer them.
3. Remain alert of changes in the marketplace that present opportunities and threats.
4. Select differentiation strategies based on the information you acquire and that reflect your unique purpose and vision.

With the proper approach, being different will allow librarians to provide outstanding value to patrons well into the future, no matter what changes it brings. Differentiation will also focus librarians' sense of purpose while sharpening creative skills—activities that will further sustain resilience to competitive threats. While largely uncertain, the future is bound to be competitive. Be ready for it by being different.

Sources for Additional Research

Christensen, C., S. Cook, and T. Hall. 2005. Marketing malpractice: The cause and the cure. Harvard Business Review 83 (12): 74-83.

> While not a discussion of differentiation per se, Cook and Hall propose a strategy for unearthing marketing opportunities by identifying the jobs customers need to get done and aligning marketing strategies to address them accordingly. This approach is useful in identifying opportunities to apply services in unique ways.

Fisk, P. 2006. *Marketing genius*. Chichester: Capstone.

> Marketing expert Peter Fisk prompts readers to challenge their creativity and imagination to understand customers and fulfill their unmet needs. The sections "Thinking What Nobody Else Has Thought," "Finding the Big Idea that Defines You," and "Seeing Business through Customers' Eyes" are particularly applicable to forming differentiation strategies. Plentiful charts, diagrams, and real-life examples make marketing concepts easy to understand for novices.

Godin, S. 2003. *Purple cow: Transform your business by being remarkable*. New York: Portfolio.

> In his usual conversational manner, popular marketing guru Seth Godin argues that marketers need another element in their marketing mix—a purple cow (a remarkable product). Throughout his book, he lists action plans ("takeaway points") and describes case studies to help organizations break through marketing clutter and draw customers to their unique product offerings.

La Piana, D. 2005. *Play to win: The nonprofit guide to competitive strategy*. San Francisco: Jossey-Bass.

> While written for traditional non-profit organizations, many of the concepts presented in LaPiana's book are relevant for libraries. The book provides worksheets and detailed directions for creating and implementing a successful competitive strategy.

Neumeier, M. 2007. *Zag: The number-one strategy of high-performance brands*. Berkeley: New Riders.

> As customers become increasingly resistant to marketing messages, Neumeier advises organizations that to stand out, they must develop qualities that are both different from the competition and worthwhile for customers, which he calls a "zag." He outlines seventeen steps, or checkpoints, for defining a zag that will lead to meaningful differentiation.

Smith, J. L. 2006. *Creating competitive advantage: Give customers a reason to choose you over your competitors*. New York: Doubleday.

> Smith's book is written for a business audience, but it presents important concepts that are necessary in understanding competitive advantage. For example, Smith distinguishes competitive advantages from strengths, and instructs readers in how to objectively define them.

Works Cited

Adamy, J. "Starbucks stirred to refocus on coffee; Strategy sharpens as chairman sends a wake-up memo." *Wall Street Journal*, February 26, 2007, eastern edition, sec. A, http://

proquest.umi.com/pqdweb?did=1222646391&sid=1&Fmt=3&clientId=4305&R
QT=309&VName=PQD.

Bell, S. 2002. New information marketplace competitors: Issues and strategies for academic
libraries. *Libraries and the Academy* 2 (2): 277-303.

Casison-Tansiri, J. 2007. Adventures in advertising: Technology helps companies create
relevancy for consumers. *Incentive* 181 (3): 9.

Chick-fil-A. 2007. Company & opportunities. http://www.chick-fil-a.com/Company.asp.

Christensen, C., Cook, S. and T. Hall. 2005. Marketing malpractice: The cause and
the cure. Harvard Business Review 83 (12): 74-83.

Correia, C. C. 2006. Libraries and competition: Intelligence for management and strategy.
Information Outlook 10 (7): 23-26.

Davidson, L. A. 1999. Libraries and their OPACs lose out to the competition. *Library
Computing* 18 (4): 279-283.

Fisher, R. J. 1991. Durable differentiation strategies for services. *The Journal of Services
Marketing* 5 (1): 19-28.

Fisk, P. 2006. *Marketing genius.* Chichester: Capstone.

Fulton, D. 2006. http://fulton.blogspot.com/2006/05/on-saturday-may-6-daveman-will-
be-at.html.

Flower, E. 2004. Competition, technology, and planning: Preparing for tomorrow's library
environment. *Information Technology and Libraries* 23 (2): 67-69.

Gibbons, S. 2001. Growing competition for libraries. *Library Hi Tech* 19 (4): 363-367.

Godin, S. 2003. *Purple cow: Transform your business by being remarkable.* New York:
Portfolio

Kim, W. C. and R. Mauborgne. 1999. Creating new market space. *Harvard Business
Review* 77 (1): 83-94.

La Piana, D. 2005. *Play to win: The nonprofit guide to competitive strategy.* San Francisco:
Jossey-Bass.

Lusch, R. F., Vargo, S. L. and M. O'Brien. 2007. Competing through service: Insights
from service-dominant logic. *Journal of Retailing* 83 (1): 5-18.

Massey-Burzio, V. 2002. Facing the competition: The critical issues of reference service.
College & Research Libraries News 63 (11): 774-775.

Neumeier, M. 2007. *Zag: The number-one strategy of high-performance brands.* Berkeley:
New Riders.

Smith, J. L. 2006. *Creating competitive advantage: Give customers a reason to choose you over
your competitors.* New York: Doubleday.

CHAPTER 13

New Training Modes for Reference Services

Jennifer Ander and Connie Strittmatter

Introduction

The previous chapters of this book have discussed new and exciting ways that reference librarians can reinvent themselves to be more relevant to our continually changing academic environment. Many of the programs and service models discussed involve both cultural and technological changes; the cultural changes require librarians to transform their services from reactive (waiting for students to approach them for help) to proactive (meeting students where they are and actively offering help), while the technological changes involve librarians learning and embracing new technologies such as wikis, blogs, and social networking tools. While these may seem like minor shifts in services, the reality is that they require a significantly different approach to staff preparation through training. Training methods must not only evolve to incorporate the change in culture and technology but also to meet the training needs of today's professionals. Some more traditional training methods, which include learning "on the fly" or listening to lectures, may not be effective. The goal of this chapter is to discuss innovative training models for new reference services, and how they address the changing roles of librarians.

Analysis of Past and Present Training Modes:

In the past, training was linear and frequently looked like this:
Lecture ➠ Demonstration ➠ Practice (Maybe) ➠ Implementation
While effective in certain situations, this paradigm lacks interactivity, self paced reviews, and refresher courses. These shortcomings can leave service providers unprepared to offer successfully new services and programs at the time of launch. Effective training is a continual process which allows an organization to be nimble and adapt to new changes to services. This shift in training acknowledges the cultural and technological changes that librarians are facing by providing them with more opportunities to acquire skills and incorporate them into their daily work practices. New models, like the one pictured in illustration 1, not only add steps to the process but incorporate new technologies (such as computer-based tutorials, gaming, video, and screen-capture software) which can aid trainees in mastering skills rather than gaining a cursory understanding of them. Because it is circular rather than linear, a learner can enter the cycle at multiple training points based on his or her learning style.

New Training Modes

Today days librarians are grappling with how to provide effective services not only at the reference desk, but also away from it. Students can be demanding—oftentimes, instant gratification is not quick enough. They are frequently

Illustration 1. New Training Models

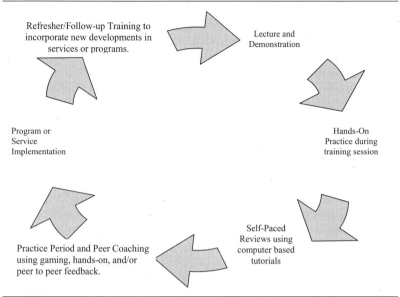

Refresher/Follow-up Training to incorporate new developments in services or programs.

Lecture and Demonstration

Program or Service Implementation

Hands-On Practice during training session

Practice Period and Peer Coaching using gaming, hands-on, and/or peer to peer feedback.

Self-Paced Reviews using computer based tutorials

technologically adept but not necessarily computer literate (Zabel, 2005, 104). To meet the service needs of these students, librarians must be flexible, adaptable, and spontaneous. In the span of a single workday, librarians may be expected to help users at the reference desk, chat with patrons online, hold office hours in academic departments, and provide roving reference.

As we offer new services to our constituents, there are four significant changes that must occur in training. Librarians need to embrace training modes that include autonomous continued training, use the social element of peer coaching, teach adaptability and flexibility, and prepare service providers to be proactive and assertive.

Autonomous Continued Training

Autonomous continued training (for example, an online, on-demand video tutorial) is useful for two reasons. It enables the organization to experiment with new technologies without the costs associated with a comprehensive program, and it encourages trainees to experiment by taking an active role in their training. Such direct involvement from the trainee is the foundation of autonomous continued training—a philosophy that focuses on train*ee*, rather than train*er*-centered learning. In this method, trainees can complete training at their own pace and repeat or skip portions depending upon their knowledge level. This training style can also be useful when services must be launched with very little time for employee training. With new technologies emerging at such a fast pace, organizations may not have time to offer formal training sessions and may opt for just-in-time training (JITT) instead (Kutzik, 2005, 8). JITT may use videos or Web-based tutorials to convey information about a new service. Employees can do these as they have time and need instead of waiting for formal training.

Some libraries are providing autonomous continued training for library staff to increase adoption of Web 2.0 technologies. While this type of training may not be directly tied to new services, library administrators see the value of having a staff well-versed in Web 2.0 technologies. An example from the public library world is the Public Library of Charlotte & Mecklenburg County (PLCMC) which has implemented the Learning 2.0 Project. Library employees are encouraged to learn and experiment with emerging technologies by completing twenty-three self-paced activities over the course of a ten-week program. Topics covered include blogging, tagging, using RSS feeds and Flickr, and downloading podcasts and videos (PLCMC). Many other libraries have adopted similar programs (Blowers and Reed, 15; LibrarianinBlack.net).

McMaster University built on PLCMC's Learning 2.0 project with Learning 2.0 @ Mac, a twelve-week program that introduces employees, students and staff to Web 2.0 technologies. This program expands upon PLCMC's in that every attendee is assigned to a learning group with a team leader. The purpose of the groups is to provide an arena for the exploration of ideas and for feedback and encouragement (About Learning 2.0 at Mac).

Streaming video can be a valuable delivery medium for autonomous continued training. Short instructional videos can be created to demonstrate how a service or program can be provided. While YouTube has been used primarily for student training up to this point, librarians are beginning to use it as a tool for staff training. A librarian at Georgia State University has created YouTube videos to teach staff how to operate the microforms machines (Jones 2007), and librarians at Murdoch University and Ricoh Innovations, Inc. have created videos to introduce librarians to providing services in Second Life (Greenhill 2007, Fairgrove 2007).

Since YouTube is publicly accessible, these videos and others like them can be shared by many libraries; instead of creating a new training program about microforms or Second Life, trainers can distribute links to videos already posted on YouTube.

Publicly posted streaming videos, online tutorials, and JITT resources allow trainees to review content at a time convenient to them and at their own learning pace. These materials can be effective training tools, but should not be the sole method of training; it is still very important to allow time for hands-on practice before a program or service becomes part of a reference team's repertoire.

Peer Coaching
Peer coaching is an effective means for staff to acquire new skills and gain experience with the support, positive reinforcement, and technical feedback from peers. Learning 2.0 @ Mac is an example of a training program which incorporates the concept of peer coaching to insure that knowledge acquired during training is

retained. When individuals learn a new skill, there is often a dip in performance before improvement is shown. During this time, trainees tend to focus on what they are doing wrong, become frustrated, and discontinue using the learned skills. Peer coaching helps trainees through this "performance dip" by providing positive reinforcement for tasks done well and feedback on areas that can be improved (Joyce and Showers, 1983). For example, by practicing online chat with colleagues, librarians can become adept at the particulars of the medium. This interactive element is one reason why allowing time for practice and peer coaching is effective and important as a technique.

Training for Adaptability and Flexibility:
When providing services to students, librarians must be able to transition smoothly from traditional to virtual to roving reference in order to deal effectively with the unique demands of each setting. For example, a librarian working at a reference desk will use a different communication and instruction method than when working with a patron in a virtual environment, or when providing roving reference. In many instances when a new service is launched, librarians are learning and implementing multiple skills, and training must accommodate these various scenarios. Norwich University librarian Meredith Farkas has experimented with "embedding" supplemental library services in WebCT courses (Farkas 2008). Before she (or any service provider) could begin to use the message boards, chat capabilities, and file upload capabilities offered by WebCT (and other courseware systems) she had to gain an understanding of those features and become comfortable using them. Only after this comfort level was achieved could she begin to provide reference and research assistance.

Organizations and companies are also turning to Web-based communities like Second Life for education and training because they are interactive and encourage experimentation in a safe environment (Training Simulations in Second Life). Companies are using Second Life to practice sale pitches, improve customer service, and provide meeting forums. For example, IBM employees log into Second Life weekly to attend training presentations, talk with customers, and hold meetings (Galagan 2008, 36). The training IBM employees receive through this medium is beneficial because it allows employees to build familiarity with technology skills and encourages them to interact in non-traditional settings. Though this innovative concept has not yet become common in academic libraries, it could easily be applied to them as well. By creating a presence in Second Life, librarians can become more comfortable with instant messaging and other virtual communication methods and understand how their users act in a virtual world.

Training for Proactivity and Assertiveness
Many new library services require a change from the "wait and see" approach that has marked some aspects of reference work as done at a reference desk. Roving, proactive, field, and embedded reference all require a greater degree of assertiveness than traditional reference services. For many institutions, this is a

major cultural change, and many librarians may be hesitant to embrace proactive reference services because they feel uncomfortable or concerned they will be perceived as invading student spaces. However, the shift to proactivity can be achieved. Numerous academic libraries have begun experimenting with more proactive approaches to reference. Because these approaches require librarians to "go where their users are" instead of waiting for them to seek assistance, they necessitate not only a shift in attitude, but also a change in the way that questions are answered. In order to rove effectively, librarians need to be comfortable using more assertive measures to approach students, know how to use a laptop or PDA, and still be able to answer questions. Though the literature addresses the importance of training, little about how to train for roving or field reference has been published over the past two decades. A spate of articles on assertiveness training for libraries was published in the 1980s, but very few of them referred specifically to academic libraries (Assertiveness 1984, Caputo 1985, Hanson Sibley 1989). Some anecdotal information is available on public e-mail lists and blogs; for example, Palm Beach Atlantic University has been offering roving only reference since its new building opened in early 2007. Librarians there trained themselves to overcome the intimidation factor of a "cold approach" through a trial and error self-training system,[1] but other libraries have documented more thorough roving training techniques. For example, Columbus Metropolitan Public Library, which also chose to eliminate its reference desk and provide roving-only services, provides more training program tips that can be adapted by academic libraries. In this case, training for assertiveness in roving included defining proactive reference, tying it to goals and objectives, dispelling related myths, and implementing pilot programs (Korenowsky 2007).

In the previous section, the concept of using the virtual environment Second Life for technology training was presented; it could also be used as a way to gain experience with proactive reference service. Libraries wanting to implement roving reference in their physical libraries could practice or role-play in Second Life, since using an avatar to approach faculty and students virtually can be less intimidating than approaching them in person. Trainees could either approach actual patrons or role-play with other librarians and staff. This practice can be beneficial in many ways; not only does it help librarians to learn new skills for use in their physical libraries, but it also provides experience in virtual environments that their libraries may choose to adopt as service points.

Conclusion

This is a time of experimentation and exploration not only for new services, but for new training modes to support librarians in designing and delivering those new services. Training is critical, yet it is often overlooked in new service implementation. Today reference teams need adequate training to build confidence in working with new services and technologies. Just as reference services and programs are changing, so too must the training that supports and accompanies these programs. Since many of these new services require flexibility and spontaneity, training must also be flexible. Sometimes it will include autonomous continued training, sometimes it will involve peer-coaching, and sometimes just-in-time training will be the most effective avenue for preparing staff. Moving from an information-centered to a user-centered model of reference requires innovation in both services and the training avenues used to supplement them. New approaches to training can provide that preparation and confidence in one's own skills and abilities and confidence in the new tools for next generation reference work.

Sources for Additional Research

Blowers, H. and L. Reed. 2007. The C's of our sea change: Plans for training staff, from core competencies to Learning 2.0. *Computers in Libraries* 27 (2): 10-15.

Realizing the importance of technological training, PCLMC implemented several new training models. This article reviews not only the Learning 2.0 project at PLCMC but also discusses their information technology core competencies. The four tiered program covers competencies such as basic e-mail, Internet, word processing skills, specialized software, and how to image computers. Each tier builds upon the foundations learned in tier 1 and is directed toward specific employee groups.

Kutzik, J. S. 2005. Just-in-time technology training for emergent needs. *Library Mosaics* 16 (1): 8-10.

Kutzik discusses the best practices for just-in-time technology training (JITT), which results when an emerging situation occurs and the timeline to implementation is very short. This article provides valuable tips on identifying a trainer, creating the program, developing training materials and evaluating the session.

PLCMC. *Learning 2.0 Project.* http://plcmcl2-about.blogspot.com/.

To encourage exploration and adoption of Web 2.0 technologies by her staff, PLCMC Technology Director Helene Blowers designed the Learning 2.0 Project. Based in part on Stephen Abram's *43 Things I (or You) Might Want to Do This Year,* the project offers incentives for staff who agree to take part. The project is implemented over a 10 week period, during which participants are encouraged to take part in personal reflection and group discussion via a personal blog as they sample freely available technologies ranging from blogs and folksonomies to photo sharing and podcasts. PLCMC's program has spawned many similar programs throughout the world.

Training simulations in Second Life. http://www.youtube.com/watch?v=DJTzNSV8pb0.

This five minute video clip provides an overview of how Second Life can be used for training and education. Examples of the types of training include exercises to measure the effectiveness of a team and how they interact with one another and role play. This video is a nice introduction to the possible ways training can be used in this virtual environment.

Works Cited

Assertiveness for Brooklynites. 1984. *Library Journal* 109 (13): 1388.

Blowers, H. and L. Reed. 2007. The C's of our sea change: Plans for training staff, from core competencies to Learning 2.0. *Computers in Libraries* 27 (2): 10-15.

Caputo, J. S. 1985. Assessment of MLA assertiveness training for librarians. Student behavior change after taking C.E. 669, Assertiveness and Human Relation Skills. *Bulletin of the Medical Library Association* 73 (4): 373-382.

Fairgrove, R. 2007. *SL Libraries – Info Insland* [sic] *Archipelago Tour*. http://youtube.com/watch?v=B8v3TZethQ0.

Farkas, M. Embedded library, embedded librarian: Strategies for providing reference services in online courseware. In *The Desk and Beyond: Next Generation Reference Services*. Eds. Sarah K. Steiner and M. Leslie Madden. Chicago: ACRL, 2008.

Galagan, P. 2008. Second that: Could Second Life be learning's second chance? *T+D* 62 (2): 34-37.

Greenhill, K. 2007. *Murdoch Uni Library Gets a Second Life*. http://www.youtube.com/watch?v=KiH7dkOVaLc.

Hanson Sibley, C. 1989. Be your best self: Assertiveness training. *School Library Journal* 35 (13): 190

Jones, J. L. 2007. *GSU Library Training*. http://youtube.com/user/gsulibrarytraining.

Joyce, B. R. and Beverly S. Showers. 1983. *Power in staff development through research on training*. Alexandria, VA: Association for Supervision and Curriculum Development, text-fiche ED240667.

Korenowsky, C. 2007. What exactly is proactive reference? Columbus Metropolitan Library Tells Its Story: So Far …. http://www.winslo.state.oh.us/newsletter/sept07cma.html.

Kutzik, J. S. 2005. Just-in-time technology training for emergent needs. *Library Mosaics* 16 (1): 8-10.

Librarianinblack.net. *Computers in libraries 2008: Technology training for library staff: Creativity works!* http://librarianinblack.typepad.com/librarianinblack/2008/04/computers-in-li.html.

McMaster University Library. *About learning 2.0 at Mac.* http://macetg.wordpress.com/about-learning-20-mac/.

PLCMC. *Learning 2.0 Project.* http://plcmcl2-about.blogspot.com/.

Training simulations in Second Life. http://www.youtube.com/watch?v=DJTzNSV8pb0.

Zabel, D. 2005. Trends in reference and public services librarianship and the role of RUSA, part two. *Reference & User Services Quarterly* 45 (2): 104-107.

Notes

1. Debora Stewart, e-mail to LIBREF-L mailing list, April 30, 2008, http://listserv.kent.edu/cgi-bin/wa.exe?A1=ind0804e&L=libref-l.

About the Editors

Sarah K. Steiner

Sarah K. Steiner is a Learning Commons Librarian at Georgia State University Library in Atlanta, Georgia, where she has been employed since 2005. She acts as Virtual Reference Coordinator, maintains the Learning Commons blog, provides research support to incoming freshmen and sophomores. She is involved with the Instruction Section of ACRL and was a member of the inaugural class of ALA's Emerging Leaders Program in 2007. Sarah received her M.A. in Library and Information Science from the University of South Florida in 2004, and is currently working on an M.A. in English Literature at Georgia State University.

M. Leslie Madden

M. Leslie Madden is the Instruction Coordinator for the University Library at Georgia State University in Atlanta, Georgia, where she has been employed since December 2005. Prior to this appointment, she served as the Humanities Librarian at the Georgia Institute of Technology in Atlanta, Georgia for eight years. She has an M.A. in English literature from Virginia Commonwealth University, and an M.S.L.S. from the University of North Carolina at Chapel Hill.

About the Contributors

Laurie A. Alexander

Laurie A. Alexander is currently the Assistant to the University Librarian at the University of Michigan. In this role, she facilitates the work of the University Librarian in a broad spectrum of administrative activities, including daily operations, writing and research, financial and personnel management, liaison to faculty and University administration, and maintaining connections to the academic and information communities beyond the University. Laurie earned her graduate degree in library science from the University of Michigan and began her professional career there in 1995 as a reference librarian at the Shapiro Undergraduate Library, later assuming responsibility for reference coordination. Most recently, Laurie served as the Interim Director of the Arts and Engineering Libraries.

Jennifer Ander

Jennifer Ander is currently employed as a Business Analyst in Spokane, WA, where she routinely puts her reference desk skills to the test. Prior to that, she worked as a Reference Librarian at Montana State University. Jennifer has also been involved with public health information education and instructional librarianship.

Chad F. Boeninger

Chad F. Boeninger is the Reference & Instruction Technology Coordinator at Ohio University's Alden Library. In his role he serves as a Reference Librarian, the Business and Economics Bibliographer and the assistant web manager. He is the creator of the *Biz Wiki* and the *Business Blog*, and is the administrator of several other blogs and wikis. He has presented and written about a variety of Web 2.0 and library technology tools such as wikis, blogs, instant messaging, open source software, podcasting, gaming, and social software. He thoroughly enjoys sharing and learning with others, and in doing so is constantly striving to make the library a viable resource for years to come. Chad shares his thoughts and ideas about libraries and technology on his blog, *Library Voice*.

Caroline Cason Barratt

Caroline Cason Barratt is a Reference and Instruction Librarian at the University of Georgia Libraries in Athens, Georgia. Her research interests include undergraduate research behavior, librarian-faculty collaboration, and assignment design. Her duties include reference and instruction at UGA's Student Learning Center, a uniquely electronic library and Learning Commons environment.

Tim Daniels

Tim Daniels is the PINES Program Manager for the PINES division of the State Library of Georgia. Previously he was the Learning Commons Coordinator for the Georgia State University Libraries. He has presented at numerous national conferences. Current job duties include managing the day to day operation for an Open Source ILS that serves 270 library facilities across the state of Georgia.

Meredith G. Farkas

Meredith G. Farkas is the Distance Learning Librarian at Norwich University in Northfield, VT. She is also an adjunct faculty member at San Jose State University's School of Library and Information Science. Meredith is the author of the book Social Software in Libraries: Building Collaboration, Communication and Community Online (Information Today, 2007) and writes the monthly column "Technology in Practice" for *American Libraries*. She also is the author of the blog Information Wants to Be Free http://meredith.wolfwater.com/wordpress/ and is the creator of Library Success: A Best Practices Wiki <http://www.libsuccess. org/> as well as a number of national conference wikis. Meredith is a passionate advocate for affordable online continuing education for librarians and developed the free online course, Five Weeks to a Social Library <http://www.sociallibraries. com/course/>, to teach librarians about social software.

Stephen Francoeur

Stephen Francoeur is an Information Services Librarian at Baruch College in New York, New York. He has published several articles about digital reference and library technology and also maintains a blog, Digital Reference, that focuses on all aspects of reference services. He is also a member of the QuestionPoint 24/7 Reference Cooperative Advisory Board.

Iris Jastram

Iris Jastram is the Reference and Instruction Librarian for Languages and Literature at Carleton College, a residential liberal arts college in Minnesota. In this position, she provides curricular research support for students in her liaison areas as well as general research assistance to the campus community as part of a joint reference and technology service point. She also blogs at Pegasus Librarian <http://pegasuslibrarian.blogspot.com/>.

Brenda L. Johnson

Brenda L. Johnson currently serves as University Librarian at University of California, Santa Barbara. From 1997-2007, Johnson was Associate University Librarian (AUL) for Public Services at the University of Michigan, University Library. As AUL for Public Services, Johnson was responsible for the leadership and direction of 19 libraries with over 200 full-time staff. Under her leadership, the Library pioneered many innovative services and programs, such as the Instructor College, Café Shapiro, Ask Us Now, and the Field Librarian Program. Johnson began her career at Michigan in 1985, serving in several positions including Head of the Social Sciences Cluster and Head of Systems Support. Preceding these appointments, she held positions at Rutgers University Libraries. Johnson holds a Master of Library Science degree from Rutgers University and a BA from Muskingum College. In addition, she attended the School of Law at SUNY Buffalo.

Ross T. LaBaugh

Ross T. LaBaugh is Coordinator of the Learning Enhancement Center at Zayed University in Dubai, U.A.E. and a Librarian at California State University, Fresno. A librarian for over 30 years, he has been actively involved with instruction and information literacy at local, regional and national levels. Ross holds degrees in English, Library Science and Professional Writing, and is a regular contributor to LOEX Quarterly. His current interests are in counseling and language acquisition.

Cliff Landis

Cliff Landis is Reference Librarian for Technology at Valdosta State University in Valdosta, Georgia. He has published and given regional and national presentations on social networking sites, Library 2.0, and the future of the Internet.

Brian S. Mathews

Brian S. Mathews is the User Experience Librarian at the Georgia Institute of Technology. He is the author of The Ubiquitous Librarian Blog, and a frequent contributor to the Designing Better Libraries Blog. Brian publishes and presents widely in the areas of marketing, assessment, and social software, and is a columnist for the *Journal of Web Librarianship*. His job duties include reference and instruction, as well as organizational and customer service assessment, brand-building, and designing academic interactions. He is currently writing a book for ALA Editions about experiential marketing. For more information, please see www.brianmathews.com.

John Russell

John Russell is a Social Sciences Librarian at the University of Oregon in Eugene, Oregon. He has previously published work on open access, U.S. labor history, French socialism, and fine printing. John is also the lead librarian for the Mana'o Project, an open access initiative for
anthropology, and editor of Bibliographica, an internationally-oriented newsletter about fine printing.

Jill S. Stover

Jill S. Stover is a Marketing Research Analyst at the Affinion Loyalty Group in Virginia. Previously she was the Undergraduate Services Coordinator at Virginia Commonwealth University's James Branch Cabell Library. She regularly writes and speaks on marketing and creativity topics, and is currently pursuing a Certificate in Marketing from the VCU School of Business. You can read more about Jill and her marketing views on her blog, Library Marketing: Thinking Outside the Book (http://librarymarketing.blogspot.com).

Connie Strittmatter

Connie Strittmatter is a Reference Librarian at Montana State University in Bozeman, Montana. Prior to joining MSU, she had worked for five years at Arizona State University as a reference librarian at Ross-Blakley Law Library and a year and a half as the director of a nonprofit public library. She is the author of "Utah Initiatives and Referenda: A Research Guide." Along with providing reference services, liaising with a variety of departments on campus and assisting with collection development, she also teaches a 2 credit course, Electronic Library Research Skills. Connie received an MLS from Kent State University in 2000 and an MBA in 2004 from the W. P. Carey School of Business at Arizona State University.

Jerilyn Veldof

As Director of Coordinated Educational Services and Undergraduate Initiatives at the University of Minnesota Libraries, Jerilyn Veldof's responsibilities include the Libraries' virtual reference service and Web usability. She has given dozens of library workshops and presentations on instructional design, usability, and performance support systems around the country and is the author of *Creating the One-Shot Library Workshop: A Step-by-Step Guide*. Her positions at Minnesota include Coordinator of User Education and Distance Learning Instruction Librarian. Prior to this she was an Undergraduate Services & Social Science Librarian at the University of Arizona Library. Jerilyn received a MLS from the State University of New York at Buffalo and a BA in Anthropology, Film, and Video at Ithaca College in New York State.

Ann Zawistoski

Ann Zawistoski is a Reference and Instruction Librarian for the Sciences at Carleton College in Northfield, MN. She offers research support for students in the sciences in both group and individual instruction sessions, as well as providing general reference at the Laurence McKinley Gould Library. She has presented at regional and national conferences, particularly on the display of visual information, and institutional repositories.